Books by Herbert Gold

Novels

Birth of a Hero
The Prospect Before Us
The Man Who Was Not With It
The Optimist
Therefore Be Bold
Salt
Fathers
The Great American Jackpot

Stories and Essays

Love and Like
The Age of Happy Problems
The Magic Will

Memoir

My Last Two Thousand Years

My Last
Two Thousand
Years

My Last
Two Thousand
Years

HERBERT GOLD

Random House　New York

Sections of this book have appeared, in other form, in *The Atlantic Monthly, Commentary, Midstream, Playboy* and *The New York Times Book Review.*

Library of Congress Cataloging in Publication Data

Gold, Herbert, 1924–
My last two thousand years

Autobiographical.
I. Title.
PS3557.034Z5   813'.5'4   72–4087

ISBN 0–394–47098–2

Manufactured in the United States of America by Haddon Craftsmen, Scranton, Pa.

First Edition

9 7 5 3 2 4 6 8

For Milik

My Last
Two Thousand
Years

In the cathedral at Palma, on the island of Mallorca, to which many Marranos fled from mainland Spain, I found menorahs wrought in gold, stars of David, Hebrew imagery in stained mosaics which had been taken as booty into the church as the captured relics of Christianity were taken into the vodun temples of Haiti. Of course, there was no Jewish community in Palma. But there were Jewish traditions. And when a prominent bullfight judge and architect discovered that his family was descended from Marranos—lost Jews— he was so filled with shock and pride that he could not keep silent; he had to speak and he had to act: honoring his past, he and his entire family left the Church to become Protestant.

The bullfight judge continued his practice of architecture, but gave up bullfight judging. "It's not in our tradition," he said haughtily.

ONE

1

By a wide and narrow road I found my way back to an allegiance I didn't possess. Born a Jew in Lakewood, Ohio, I embraced the belief and accusation: American is enough.

If that's not enough, pleasure will be enough.

And if that's not enough, art and the life of art will be enough.

Health, love, money, luck, and words will surely suffice. A community can be carved out of all the riches of America without resorting to tribal myths. Those are principles and articles of faith. Aren't they?

I set my paper zoo afire under the stove and got slapped by an aunt with disordered teeth and an accent. Broom scattering, feet stamping, a pan of water thrown on the floor. A thick wet smell of scorch. Where there had been a jungle of spiders, caterpillars, spiky edges of linoleum, tacks buried in their own rust, and a life of fire, now there was flood, invasion, death, destruction. "I said don't, but you did!"

My nightmares were of giant enemies from elsewhere—teeth, roar, huge thighs—while the lake captain's son next door bounced his ball against the wall of our house so that my brothers and I couldn't have our naps. His mother instructed him. My mother explained it to me.

A black kid was supposed to come to our school, the child of a serving couple from one of the big houses near Lake Erie. We had a day of drill in how to respond like Americans to this crisis, with dignity, loving kindness, and not too much staring, but he never showed up.

On the day the black child didn't come to school, Jack O'Shea, the lake captain's son, asked my brother and me to come home and wrestle with him. We knew his mother didn't want us in their house. We went, we wrestled, he pressed us tightly against himself, there was a smell of fireworks and punk, like the Fourth of July. We knew we had done wrong to go into this strange house. The next day Jack was up to his mother's tricks again—a steady rhythm of bouncing and bouncing a ball against our wall, slats, screens.

My friend Ferd Klabber's elder brother told me he wanted to study my folkways for an anthropology project at Adelbert College. "What's kosher? Why are you circumcised?" he asked, pencil in the air.

"So I can hold the peepee longer'n you can."

My parents thought it was time for some religious education.

I got carsick lurching the twenty miles from Lakewood to the east side of Cleveland, where the Reverend Bertrand S. Benker, Rabbi, instructed us in a Jewish Unitarianism whose main precept was: Love your neighbor as yourself and don't marry a shicksa. I had more important things on my mind, such as discovering that I was the natural son of Feodor Chaliapin, the Russian singer, and finding a girl named Lucille, gloomy and Swedish, whose real father was T. S. Eliot.

She believed me and I believed her and we practiced what

we read about in George Sylvester Viereck's history of the Wandering Jew, *My First Two Thousand Years*, which promised eventually to reveal the secret of "unendurable pleasure indefinitely prolonged." As we lay down in a cornfield, having ridden our bikes out in search of cheeseburgers and our true fathers, answers to the riddles of prose and poetry, she agreed that the distinguished German-American writer, Mr. G. S. Viereck, wrote really beautifully, throbbingly, for a novelist. She liked the whole idea about Lilith, Adam's demon first wife, who exhausted his loins—poetic. Teenage sex in a cornfield taught me that the Word is not all that is holy. Also that some writers, for example, George Sylvester Viereck, exaggerate.

Art and love were real. Religion made me carsick, and it was stupid, besides. I already loved Lucille as myself. My parents were too busy with the Store to argue with a willful son. Maybe Americans didn't have to be bar-mitzvah'd.

When Mr. Fergus, who lived on our block and owned the Toledo Theater, was arrested as a child-molester, everyone assumed he was a Jew. His son Michael and I became friends. My mother brought his mother a lemon pie in her time of trouble. Michael and I took to tennis together. Strolling toward the courts, I heard someone call out, "Deuce again!" and I trembled, hearing *Jews again.* Mrs. Fergus confessed to my mother that they were not Jewish persons and I felt betrayed by Michael—friends only because his father was a child-molester, a person of the pederastic persuasion, therefore in exile like us. I wanted to forgive him. But I no longer knew why we should be friends.

At an assembly the principal's nephew, a stocky lad named Brucie, described his happy year in the Third Reich. Racial Purity was a logical ideal. Who wants racial impurity? "I didn't see any persecution of Jews," he said. The public speaker wet his lips. "Of course, I didn't see any Jews either." Laughter.

Deuce again.

The chief sin in Lakewood was lust. The bearer of sin was the Christ-Killer. But inexorably the sap rose in healthy Lucilles, Patties, Dotties, and Susans, and they learned to feel Desire. A set of interlocking syllogisms made trouble, as strict logic often does. Sex is forbidden. Jews are sexual monsters. But we want to snake our long arms about another, we lie awake dreaming of it. To do this with a boy we might marry is an abomination, plus impractical: he'll lose respect. Bad enough to lose breath, buried against a body, without also risking future prospects. The good lads are struggling to be pure, too. Oh, dilemma.

Ergo, choose the Jew, who is already damned; and thus in league with the forces of darkness, he has experienced all the pleasures, can teach them, practice them, and direct the sadder but wiser body toward a grand repentance in the soul.

Together with Sheldon Shapiro, who lived ten blocks away, I was offered the joy I least expected. Just when we wanted to learn tennis, we had to learn soul-kissing.

Lucille moved on.

Susan asked me to work her combination. Her locker was stuck. "You're Mosaic," she said, running her hand first through her own hair and then through mine. The way she said it sounded as if I were made of little glued tiles.

"Jewish," I said stubbornly, "a Jew."

But when she touched me the little tiles fell apart.

"Your father came from . . . ?"

"The Old Country. Talks with an accent."

"I know that," she said. "It's all right." And contemplatively she bit the meaty part of my palm. "I like to bite right there. Umm, I like to bite. Is your mother the same kind of Mosaic person?"

"Jewish," I insisted. Deuce again. She couldn't get it through her head about the tiles.

"I like you a lot," she said, "you know that. Why don't you ever try anything? Do this, for instance."

2

I learned in my boyhood that I was a stranger, a gypsy. And this had its privileges: to be exotic when what was normal was dead-white, bland, and suburban. It would be wise to cultivate strangeness.

But also I saw no possible community in Lakewood. I could join neither Aunt Anna nor Lucille nor Susan, Michael Fergus nor Jack O'Shea, in more than the solidarity of a disordered moment. Family was a tight closet in which I could not breathe.

What I wanted could be discovered elsewhere, if at all.

I heard there were Jews like me toward the east and, at age seventeen, just out of high school, I set forth, past Shaker Heights to Pittsburgh and New York, by hitchhiking thumb, to work in restaurants for meals, sleep in odd places, find redeeming adventure. I spent a wanderyear traveling, sending postcards to my parents.

My father came to America from Russia and lived in a

basement on the Lower East Side. I came to America from
Lakewood to live in a basement on the Lower East Side. I
washed dishes, cleaned rooms, waited on tables, and tried to
learn a little Yiddish. In 1942 there was still an immigrant
society in those streets, men who looked and smelled like my
father. I traveled in a dazed adolescent crisis, suddenly
finding sex and Jews everywhere in the land of plenty. There
were Jewish shoeshine men and Jewish whores and Jewish
cops. I was a Jewish kid with hands smelling persistently of
grease and strong soap. I slept in the kitchen of a Rumanian
restaurant on Hester Street. I learned to drink coffee and
smoke cigarets, my eyes gritty with longing, my mouth rehearsing superior rejoinders, my heart reconstructing my
tragic past (Lucille, Susan, Lakewood, the unendurable midwest indefinitely prolonged). When the winter got too cold,
and my hands were peeling and swollen, I hitchhiked southward. In Philadelphia I was picked up by a drunken Buick
dealer who was escaping his wife and children, escaping his
life, and he needed someone to drive so he could drink and
talk and forget. Now I was a Jewish chauffeur. I was also a
seventeen-year-old Jewish psychiatrist.

When he also needed a boy to make love to, I left him in
Georgia. A bit of jail, picking the sheriff's peaches, then some
odd jobs in Florida and Key West, scraping the cradlecap off
my head. At the end of this season, I came home to ruminate
upon my gains, if any.

A firm hand was required to call me to order. "Okay, smar-
tie, now you're home, time to go to college," my mother said.
"The best school in the country, a great law school, a great
medical school, it's right here in Cleveland, it's Western Reserve University. Everybody says it's the best. Murray's going, Stanley's going. You can have your own room at home."

"I'm going to Columbia in New York."

"What, you crazy? Pay all that money to live in New York?"

"That's where I'm going."

"Your father," said my mother, "did all he could to get away from New York. Why do you smoke? Why do you drink so much coffee? You're crazy."

"Right. I'm going to Columbia."

"We can't afford it."

"I have a scholarship."

"How do you know?"

"They told me."

"Do you believe them?"

It turned out, in the words of the report in my file, that the Dean of Admissions had written: "Admit this boy, but no financial aid. Enough Jews from New York without importing them from the midwest." It had been a mistake to expect a scholarship. It was a mistake for my advisor to let me hold the file in my lap while he answered the telephone.

When I heard about the no-scholarship, I said, "I'm going anyway."

"It don't make sense."

"I'll work. I can get a meal job, I can get a job on a switchboard."

"Good to work, good for a kid, but at Western Reserve you won't have to work. All your time for being a doctor, a lawyer. You can have your own room. You can use the car. You can date girls in the car."

And so I headed east toward Columbia. My mother gave me a basket of chicken and tomatoes and a jar of prunes to take on the Greyhound. She feared anti-Semitism and constipation on the new Pennsylvania Turnpike. From what she knew of me, she suspected I would push on even if Cossacks, hoofs pounding, muskets crackling, rode down onto the

13

Howard Johnson rest stop from the wild Alleghenies near Harrisburg. She also feared for my digestion, my soul, and my future as a lawyer-doctor away from Western Reserve University, the vital center of American learning, where Murray Poston and Stanley Strassberg were making their mothers very, very happy.

I hid the basket of food under the seat so I could eat greasy sandwiches and grainy milk shakes like everyone else. On that bus leaving the midwestern plain which ends in Cleveland, entering the gentled rolling and lurching of the roads carved through the Allegheny Mountains, I tried to take stock of my ignorance and fish some understanding out of the flood of childhood which still carried me along like a chip in a stream. These Greyhound strangers seemed closer to me than all our neighbors on the silent streets of Lakewood; the welter of heat from dozing flesh was what I craved, a welter of cities to fill the empty isolation of the suburb. The easiness of graded roads through mountains made the bus heave like a ship through the same mile-high waves and currents of the North Atlantic which had brought my father westward to America. It was night and I was voyaging into that Manhattan which meant a confused life of learning, love, and art. Through a shrieking dark tunnel on the Pennsylvania Turnpike I remembered that Jewry also inhabited New York, and I was crawling toward it through these tunnels, and it would be different—tiles flashing by, then starlight in the east— from Hadassah and Hillel and that Unitarian Reformed Temple of Cleveland. Since I was now wandering, I considered the wanderings of my ancestors.

My wandering also brought me into the belly of America, where I could do anything, the freedom of art, the freedom of self-creation in the image and pattern of nobody else. Trains, planes, buses, and motorcycles always give another message besides the sensible one: here is transportation. By my side, the warm flesh shifting in the rhythm of wheels and motor was part of the promise of new places. I couldn't make out her face, but her body slid near my shoulder and leg. I would try not to think about her; instead, I would consider the meaning of my life; I would think about her in that way.

Friendship and family had been the only community of my boyhood, and in my suburban longing for more, I imagined that love and art would make the deeper connections with others that I craved. Temperament, not intention, led my fate, which seemed odd for the writer and philosopher I fancied myself. Temperament and unexamined impulse also seemed to move others; we poet-thinkers, illegitimate sons and daughters of Feodor Chaliapin and T. S. Eliot, were like everyone else.

I imagined that to be a member of the society of Jewry might have magical significance for me, as it seemed to have for the anti-Semites I knew, even though I knew myself to be a Jew and unmagical. The bar mitzvah I had rejected was a momentous lack of occasion, a place of silence in history louder than the catered parties for other boys which I later attended. To turn away from the Jews, that elsewhere people, seemed a way to join the life of general truth, poetry, knowledge. In my confusion and fear, this was my idea. Art and knowledge were real, not tribal reversions. I was much afraid, though fear took the form of expectation that I might win the world. The emptiness of history in Lakewood did not give shape to my longings, but it provided needs which made me move and released my energies. I lived by my adolescent sufferings—but didn't even have them every day.

How to become a man in the suburb of Lakewood? What rites of car, hamburger, dance, and date served for others? Fumbling with a girl's blouse. Beginning a savings account.

They didn't serve for others, either, but especially they didn't serve for me.

Under leafy Cleveland trees I had walked off my adolescent insomnias, feeling immortal because I didn't sleep nights (in fact, I often slept mornings, instead), and knew despite my convictions of omnipotence that I was only I and no one else. It was not enough to be omnipotent and alone. Through my desire to make a friend of the child-molester's son, I knew I wanted to become a friend of criminals; I wanted to join the tribe of artists, of outcasts, perhaps even the community of my ancestors. I was a Jew and there were others someplace. In New York this tribe of strangers to whom I belonged had gathered. I was I, but not only I. There was also a center to be discovered.

And yet I could do nothing yet to join this imagined family. Lakewood was the only home I knew; I clung to it. Leaving Lakewood, I sought love, which meant the common sap of my own body, and felt only the community of the girl jiggling in the dark on the seat of the bus next to me, breathing gum.

Since I was a poet and thinker, I could do anything. Smelling Juicy Fruit, I smelled lust, souls touching, adventure, a shared mystery, powdered and flavored sugar. I dozed and awakened to find a girl in the dark of Pennsylvania who had let her head fall onto my shoulder. I touched her hair and she grabbed me astonishingly. Skinny and wriggly, she was full of tricks. This was life! And I hadn't even seen Van Am Quad yet.

When the lights went on for the next comfort stop, near Harrisburg, this delicious obscene girl had left Shangri-la to become as old as my mother. Oh, pain. Streaked iron-gray hair and a barn of a mouth full of tooth debris. She sat at one stool and I sat at another, both eating stamped-out porkburgers. Indigestion and indignation, but at least sex takes a firm hold, once a fellow leaves Cleveland. There was better to look forward to, if I could only escape trichinosis.

However, Hartley Hall, the dorm at Columbia, provided no remedy for the claims of lust on Morningside Heights. I found myself in love with a girl who haunted the Columbia Chemists, eating b-l-t's, hold the mayo; but so was everybody else in love with Peggy, and so was Peggy. All the joy I had received of Lucille and Susan came to naught in Manhattan. I was a kid from Lakewood who knew nothing. I took to philosophy, Greek myths, humanities, contemporary civilizations, Beethoven quartets, fanatical psychologies, and heart-to-heart talks. We neglected politics because there was a war on and we would soon see it for ourselves.

I also discovered art movies. This meant foreign languages at the Thalia, *Un Carnet de Bal, Grande Illusion,* and the original *M.* Also *Chapayev* (Russian), *Ordet* (Danish), and cautious Warner Brothers warnings against chain gangs, Nazism, and brain tumors. The Apollo Theater on 42nd Street was cheap, easy to reach by subway, and open during the hours when I should have been studying. In 1942 it cost fifteen cents in the early afternoon. The expense, plus the subway nickel, could be amortized by taking a meal in the cafeterias of Times Square: lasagna, eggplant parmigiana, or chopped liver on rye, cheaper than at the Columbia Chemists.

I was alone in the Apollo one afternoon, seeing *Poil de Carotte;* there was this boy, later killed in the war, and Harry Baur, later killed by the Germans, but I remember little about the film except pastures, peasants, soft notations about a Better Time, and the thought that, well, it was improving to my French. I was sitting alone in the nearly empty theater. There was a mood of wheat fields, flowing grain; and then there was a hand on my knee.

17

A glow of teeth, a darkly pomaded head, and firm claws on my leg.

What flashed through my freshman brain was a mélange of Plato, Freud, Hartley Hall exchange of news, refreshed liberalism, and pure terror. Understand the man's problem. He was lonely and went to the movies in the afternoon because he needed human companionship. I should recall Gide, Alcibiades, Jack O'Shea, and that grad student in philosophy who helped me with my French. I should be comprehensive. I moved away.

So did he. He moved away—toward me. I moved to another seat. So did he. He followed me happily, grinning, with fingers filed by sharpened intentions.

At last I burst out, forgetting culture, "Take your hands off me!"

A pair of puppet heads turned toward us across the aisle, and then, registering a mild weather condition, turned back to the screen. Nothing new for the Apollo.

The man sighed softly and moved, crouching, down the row and out, under the mote-filled beam of light, while Harry Baur took that soon-to-be-dead boy's head in his arms to comfort him for some obscure hurt, perhaps only because he had red hair.

I watched the rest of the movie with a specious alertness and attention. Inside I was bulging with shame. I had committed an intolerant act; I had been illiberal; I was a disgrace to the art of seeing movies alone at the Apollo.

The film ended, and unless I wanted to sit through it again, I had to leave. A rustle and shuffle of departing customers. In fact, I wanted to go; the place was spoiled; instead of releasing me from self-consciousness, it had given me things to think about.

Outside, Times Square would be boiling with early evening—neon, vendors, servicemen, and the war news. Suddenly I wanted to be back home in Lakewood, back home in Hartley Hall, back home anyplace. But my duty was not yet done.

I pushed past the seats, raising the ones which bumped my knee, like a good citizen. I sniffed sour salty buttered popcorn, sickish pop, the ammoniac drift of urinal scents. In the lobby, beneath the Coming Attractions of a crusading prison exposé with Paul Muni, I found an unexpected friend, that homeless soul whom I had brutally turned away. Somehow he had become an old man in my mind, but when I saw him in the light, he was young again, only a few years ahead of me, with sleek cheeks, sulky mouth, and hooded eyes. The eyes narrowed as I approached to do my duty. He leaned against a poster of Jean Gabin in *Quai des Brumes*. I said, "I'm sorry if I was rude—"

He nodded encouragingly.

"You have every right, I suppose, to do what you want to do, but it's just that I'm not—"

He waited. He would hear me out.

"Anyway, I want you to know that personally I have no objection to your doing what you want to do, it's a matter of opinion, but I personally—"

I was nervous, liberal, equivocating, and guilty.

He said, "Fuck off, Buster."

3

Most of the freshman class enlisted in the spring of 1943, as we turned eighteen. In Air Force basic training my friend Morgan Delaney, the poet and drill corporal, wondered if I shouldn't be transferred to infantry replacement. He showed me his journal as evidence for his reasoning: after the war those Jews with combat medals would have earned the respect of honest men. Only bigots would hate Jewish heroes. We drilled on land reclaimed from an Atlantic City garbage dump by a layer of black ashes and gravel. When the sun shone hot and we lay collapsed in ten-minute breaks, we got drunk off the alcohol fumes wisping up from impacted trash. When skin touched this odd terrain, some of us got lye burns—fat and rinds filtered through sunbaked ash.

Morgan Delaney, aged twenty, hair bleached white, nose peeling, was an old man of deep feeling and an artist. He liked me for my quick responses. His own kind didn't understand him so well. Off duty, we strolled the boardwalk and he told me about his future history as a famous poet, the interior walls of his historical southern mansion covered with framed letters from reformed suicides, crowned heads, grateful millionaires, sensitive ghetto children, and beautiful but unhappy ladies whose paltry lives he had enriched and somehow redeemed. He had a wife whom he loved as only a poet could love. I couldn't possibly understand that, but a real man and poet doesn't tell about the incredible things a poet's wife does to him in the sack. I'd just have to use my imagination.

We clattered in boots on the splayed and splintered boardwalk which followed the Atlantic shore for a mile or two. The town looked like a garage, dust-covered for the duration. The hotels were blacked out at night against enemy submarines. A few insomniac vacationers carried flashlights to pick their way against obstacles, spy on neckers, or discover Nazi saboteurs as they fled dripping ashore. I listened to the lapping of the sea, that same dark sea in which men were really dying, and wondered why I accepted friendship with Morgan, rather than just going to the movies or eating chocolate malts with my fellow trainees. Because he was a white-haired poet. Because he declared that we were brothers despite that I was a foreigner, with an inscrutable soul or maybe no soul at all, burdened with both secrets and blindness. Because if he turned against me, his friend in headquarters would have me transferred to infantry replacement.

He told me about racial memory and Jungian dreamsouls. He showed his interesting yellowish teeth. He reminded me that he would never discuss his wife's illicit madness sexual practices, not even with me.

I sought friendship, avoided risks. George Sylvester Viereck, the author, my early inspiration and the distinguished Nazi propagandist, was in prison again for wrong comments. Difficult times. And as to Morgan's wife, I was sure that every love is unique to the lover. That's a truth which I had already noticed. Love is linked with everything a fellow could think of.

Temporarily surfeited with intimacy and literature, we went to look at the war map in the day room of our squadron. Hitler advanced on all fronts. Stalingrad was a goner for sure.

Inductees killed time, chewing gum, sucking Milky Ways. Morgan recalled that my sort is good to children, real family folks, but we don't understand romantic passion in the Christian and southern tradition.

On the map, the anti-Christian Communist red thumbtacks were trying to stop the non-Christian Nazi black thumbtacks at the Volga, or if not there, in the white steppes of unholy Russia. I defended myself by hinting at the deep passions of Lakewood, but followed his example of southern tact by avoiding those episodes of crusty drive-in underwear.

"Maybe you should meet my wife," Morgan said. "She would find you very interesting, I'm sure, just as I do."

As a new win-the-war measure, acting drill corporals were assigned to kitchen duty. Morgan joined me in a confusion of steam, soap, lye, and rasping cleansers, watched over by the baleful grease-encrusted eyeballs of mess noncoms. We suffered this together. Ah, my friend. "At least it's an experience," I said.

I was unworldly, out of touch, a false prophet. "It's an experience for ten minutes," he said. "After that it's redundant."

There was a half hour between meals when we stretched out on the slats next to the overflowing GI cans. We smoked, watching for rats, and dropped off to sleep in the dense and humid back-alley sun until a boot stirred us and it was time to heave ourselves into the cauldron of another mass feed. Morgan was right. We had gotten all the good out of it already. Back down the alley that night after work, the world had left us behind, the day had disappeared in grease and soap, steam and abuse, and we crawled into our bunks. Awful loneliness, nobody to protect us, and a bone ache like a prediction of age and the despair of youth.

"There's something I've been meaning to talk to you about," Morgan said.

I thought we had been talking about what he meant to talk with me about. I wanted to sleep and start afresh, absent from kitchens.

"A favor. I hope you don't mind—"

What southern courtesy. What savoir-vivre.

"But I'll mention it some other time. There's something else—my father. He's coming to visit me. He's still sore I didn't go to OCS, so I told him about you, the much more interesting people a poet meets in the ranks, and he wants to take you to lunch next Sunday."

"*Me?*"

"Not just you, me too."

Relief. A new Russian defeat didn't make me as queasy in the belly as the image of a table alone with Morgan's father, the southern aristocrat and newspaper publisher.

"Of course, I could eat in the mess hall and meet you afterwards—"

"My friend. *He wants to take you to lunch.*"

I, too, needed to learn some savoir-vivre. I would break bread with a sophisticated leader in the field of regional journalism.

Morgan's father was like no father of mine, neither Feodor Chaliapin nor my real father. In the discreet mass of curly gray hair, the healthy cheek with high dark shaving, the heavy, ironic, and sensual mouth, I identified easy southern grace. There it was. No doubt great success with women. No doubt my friend Morgan took after his mother in his pale peeling skin, tremendous soul. "So you're my son's friend," Mr. Delaney said, "the friend of the son of my first wife."

Well, it was a family which liked careful classification. Mr.

Delaney's feudal princery (four newspapers, all in the Carolinas), enabled him to live part of the year in New York and, before the war, in Europe. Maybe there was a secret in Paris which explained Morgan's concentration on the ideal of love. When Mr. Delaney smiled upon me, with great savoir-vivre, the truth suddenly flashed clear and complete in my head: he had a Jewish dancer from the Folies Bergère stashed away in an apartment in occupied Paris! I could see her as clear as I saw heaven—dark ringlets, a consumptive wheeze when she laughed, a skinny terrier to burrow in laps. My amazing clairvoyance was undimmed by K.P.

Otherwise, how to explain the fond fatherly concern with which he asked, "Ever eat steamed clams, son?"

"No." O Fifi, it's you who is responsible for this buttery hot pleasure.

"That's what I thought. Your people doesn't prefer to eat clams, does it?"

"I guess it's like pig," I said, thinking, I guess you're a little like your son the way you say, *Your people* . . .

"Well, I don't suppose you prefer to stay innocent of steamed clams."

"Sounds delicious." I was eager to graduate from chocolate malts to more cosmopolitan indulgence. I wondered if lightning would strike or, perchance, stomach distress.

The pierside restaurant, windows hung with wartime blackout curtains, gleamed inside with cutlery, napkins, fishy-eyed busboys, ancient gentlemen in broad-beamed waiter's aprons, and sweating eaters who were evidently condemned to death and taking their last meals. There was utter concentration on shellfish. We, on the other hand, inspired by Morgan's father, remained an island of suavity amid crustacean greed. Mr. Delaney questioned me about family, Lakewood, college, the Army, my future. His curiosity about his son's friend and Fifi's cousin overcame a normal concentration on higher thoughts and lower appetites. The steamed clams arrived. I found them tasting like cutlets of celestial butter, and found this taste good. I began to sweat like the others, spearing, dipping, sipping, discarding shells in a gritty plate; the heap in the bucket dwindled. My pleasure was extreme, but I caught Morgan's eye in its mysterious pale calculation. I would repay him somehow.

The slight stomach ache from too many steamed clams differs from the deep-sea bends of prolonged exposure to the Army's raisin pie. One is mainly warm distention, the other, well, a knotty weight. Healthy clams are distinct from impacted raisins. I learned all this and more on that evening of elegance.

Mr. Delaney held my hand a long time when he shook goodbye, gazed deeply into my eyes, smiled more winsomely than ever. He thanked *me* for an outstanding evening. Oh, Cousin Fifi in Paris. I don't know how I knew.

The lamps along the boardwalk were painted black. It was early spring, and dusk already. Maybe a submarine was landing somewhere up the Jersey shore, Nazi saboteurs scurrying across marshes in search of guttural-voiced gas-station operators to supply them with counterfeit ration coupons and road maps to Washington. A few oldsters strolled near the beach, eerily lit by the glow of ocean minerals. The lap-lapping of waves was a recent passion. In that sea, clams waited to be steamed for men who knew how. I had drunk too much white wine. I slept on my feet before I got to the hotel, and traveled through the next day in a euphoric headache.

"Dad liked you," Morgan said. "You're a fine young man without any pushiness. You listened to his stories."

"Especially about the dancer in Paris."

His pink face looked puzzled. "What? I don't remember that one."

"Oh yeah, yeah, I was thinking of somebody else."

He stared. This was the first time I had met a civilian and eaten steamed clams. What someone else? his look asked. Some rabbi sneaking me home for a glimpse of his heavy-lidded daughter penned away from the USO?

Morgan cleared his throat. "Jews commit white-collar crimes, don't they?" he asked. "Hate trouble, don't they? Hate violence?"

Now it was coming. Morgan wanted to correspond with me in the infantry. Although he enjoyed our milk shakes together, heads together over the fascinating intricacies of his journal—a fine mind struggling for the Truth in an anti-Jungian Air Force—he could also imagine writing long confiding letters to me in some APO where I fought like a man. He would miss me a lot. But in the infantry I would learn what life is really like. Fortunately, with his poet's insight, he already knew.

And yet, if he liked me enough (I thought), he would want to keep me around. Narrowly I measured his mood.

"I could get you sent," he was saying. "That's not a threat, Herb. Don't think of it as a threat. Actually, it would be a favor. But I could get you transferred, no point in a healthy young city fellow like you wasting away in an easy flyboy job . . ."

"I don't mind."

"You ought to wake up. You ought to see the real America, blood and killing, Herb. You ought to go against your inherited style."

"You mean kill?"

"Take your chances," he said.

"I already ate steamed clams. How many more chances you want me to take? What's on your mind?"

He hadn't really cleared his throat. Now he was really doing it.

"Next weekend," he said, "mmm mmm mmm meant to ask you, next weekend, if you don't mind, I mean, next weekend . . . my wife . . ."

"That's wonderful!"

"But I'm scheduled for K.P. The bastards. That's where I am on the roster."

I was dull-witted from all the kitchen grease and lye my brains had been soaked in, the marches, classes, and extra duty my slouching nature had inflicted upon me. Basic training gave us that crowded, claustrophobic feeling which is its purpose—crowd out past, future, intentions, judgments, in favor of doing what comes easiest. Obey, stubbornly obey. But the civilian soldier keeps thinking he should be doing something else—sleeping, say, or staring at the sea—and so finds himself on the double, hup hup hup, doing the dishes.

"Would you?" he was asking. There were papery edges of skin on the flanges of his nose. Sunburned again.

"Unh?"

"Are you with me, pal? My wife. They'll put you on the duty roster for me. They'll do that for us both."

How glad I was in my heart for his long leisurely day with his bride, drinking white wine and eating steamed clams between bouts of marvelous sex. And how sorry in my heart, soul, brain, and limbs, and in my chapped hands, that his clam-eating was to be at the price of my immersion in the chaos of the kitchen, when I should be healing my soul on my first three-day pass, on the train into Philadelphia, where I could drink thick malts at the Philly USO. Well, it would be an experience.

A dizziness of grease, heat, clank of trays, grunts and shoves of my kitchen masters. I had washed civilian dishes in restaurants in New York and Florida, but this was different. I emerged stunned after eighteen hours to an invitation to dine with Morgan Delaney and his lady. The note was on my bunk. I stood in the hot shower, soaking, evolving back up the evolutionary scale, and then went to meet them at their sidestreet hotel. My suntans were clean, but there were wrinkles. It seemed important to me. My heart was pounding as if it were my own sidestreet wife I was meeting, Lucille or Susan, my love, my life. I couldn't understand why I was so worried. After what I had sacrificed for their lovemaking, my nicked and swollen hands, my red-rimmed eyes, my maddened and confused ears, I should have been confident of their friendship. When I asked the clerk, "What room? Mr. and Mrs. Delaney?" my voice shook.

The desk clerk was an overage geezer with a wrecked nose. "Who are you, soldier?"

As if it were some sour orgy we were planning, not included in the cost of rooms in the Beach (non-beach) Hotel.

"Room 401. They're expecting you, Private."

She was not a thrilling girl. She seemed intelligent. She looked like an Indian. I thought those three things while I said hello and she put out her soft, thin, bony hand and held mine warmly a moment. She was perched on the edge of an atrociously mussed bed.

"Hello," she said, "I'm Kim. Morgan has told me so much about you. I feel I know you"—but despite these ancient phrases from a book of etiquette, she didn't smooth down her skirt. She was easy with herself. Her dark narrow eyes were slightly bloodshot, but there was that keen Indian look, black straight hair, and her sallow skin was nearly the color of her lips. She looked at me as if she liked me. I still felt the silken skin of her hand in mine. She had a number of brownish moles on her cheeks. I forgave her. I had suffered a weekend in the kitchen so they could muss this bed. Like suddenly being driven to the edge of a cliff and pushed off, I fell dizzily in love. And with no hope, just waited to break below.

"I'm trying to get a job in New York," she was saying. We must have been conversing. "In publishing," she said.

"That way," Morgan explained—he had spoken before, but I had seen and heard nothing but Kim—"that way she can help my career by showing my poems to the people who really care about poetry. And can do something about making a poet known in the field. You know who I mean, Herb. They control publishing."

"Morgan, that's not it at all," she said. "Morgan, that's silly. Herb, why don't you come out for a nice stroll on the board-walk with us. I have to catch my train in a couple of hours, and we can't just sit in this, this *room.*"

Morgan looked hatred at me.

"No thanks," I said, "why don't I just come back and say goodbye to you later?"

"Oh, please do, we've been all alone here for days now."

"I've got some things," I said, "um, straighten up for inspection."

I had nothing to do but to avoid Morgan's glare. He hated me no less for leaving. He had wanted me to admire her, but he was a jealous man, it seemed.

"Come see us at the station. Come say goodbye," he called as I left, and before I could get to the stairway I heard her little shrieks as he began to beat her.

I ran back up. In my confusion I only listened in that musty hallway. I remembered "the unwritten law." It was not only unwritten, but also I had no idea what it was about. Maybe a man had the right to beat his wife. Not having been married, how could I judge? It was more like scratches, kicks, pokes than the sullen lower-class thumpings I had heard about. But I couldn't stand listening—shouts, squeals, the cry "Don't! don't!" I ran away.

The old geezer at the desk stared as I fled through the lobby. In his time the fun lasted longer.

Can it be that I bought a box of salt-water taffy as a souvenir of Atlantic City, N.J.? That's what I next remember.

At the train for Philadelphia, Baltimore, and points south, Morgan stood with his wife wearing a face older than his father's, reddened with sunburn and swollen with tears. He was weeping for his love. She had a blackened eye, a bruised cheekbone. She would leave him now. He was sobbing uncontrollably. The war would go on, we would go on to war, but she was finished with him. He clung to her, sobbing like a woman. Her mind was made up. She was straight and vigorous despite her injuries. She was part Cherokee, he had told me, and now I believed him. She patted his arm. Be brave, my dear, be brave. His face was crinkled like a child's mug, exhausted with weeping. She was smiling and waving. The train was moving. She smiled. She waved.

Morgan turned to me. "Come back and let me show you my journal," he said. For this I did his kitchen work? To give him some interesting entries? "If it weren't for keeping things straight," he said. "I don't know where I'd be."

The next week, orders transferred me to an infantry unit, the Hundredth Division, now training at Fort Bragg. Morgan had personally selected me for the roster. He was proud of my future as a BAR man, carrying an automatic rifle into fire from Germans who, after all, as Colonel Lindbergh pointed out, were really only interested in killing Jews. The poet was proud. Things had a certain appropriateness, which is what poets like. A musical logic, a rhythmical, mythic, Yeatsian, Jungian logic; it all went into his journal, which I read with genuine interest. He was also touched by the danger which brushed us all. On the whole, it was an exciting war filled with curious fates.

I admired and envied his passion and his stupidity. He became a famous poet. I admire him still.

4

"Rool down those sleeves, soldier."

I stood up. "Roll them?"

"*Sir.* And stand up. And rool down those sleeves rat away now!"

I shambled to my feet in the luncheonette where I was drinking a milk shake with a girl from the University of North Carolina whom I had met because she was carrying a record of *Strange Fruit* sung by Billie Holiday, as a sign that she wanted to meet a northern liberal, aged about nineteen— me. I drank this milk shake with my khaki sleeves rolled up because it was so hot. I also wanted to show the round-headed little music lover my mighty forearms, who I was, the *real me*, and these unmilitary bared forearms gave me identity and soul. Surely I wanted myself to know the real me, too.

Lieutenant Johns, a pimply pink shortie of a man, very narrow bones, ROTC at Harvard, had a new habit of saying "rool" for "roll" and "rat away" for "jump when I say jump." He was looking for his own soul as an officer in North Carolina. A Harvard man who didn't like college kids, one of his roles in life (rools?) was to torment me. In my self-absorption I failed to notice that he didn't like anyone.

He looked at the girl and barked, "Stand up strat."

"I can't because my knees hit the table. This here is a booth, sir," I said. My military career was teaching me the Stepin Fetchit shamble, a way of gefuffling upon power until it collapses beneath the weight of cunning incompetence.

"Come on out chere, soldier. Rat now! On the double!"

I scrambled up while the girl clutched her Billie Holiday record to her breasts. I was the fighting street kid, the desperate thinker, the big city tough from the north. And here in Fayetteville I slumped like a craven sharecropper being given the landlord treatment.

"Now stand up strat, soldier." Lieutenant Johns came close and peered with his pinkish eyes at the knot of my tie. He fingered it to make sure it wasn't hiding an undone shirt button. He said, "This knot is pretty loose, soldier."

He was handling my neck. I couldn't touch him. "May I sit down now, sir?" I asked.

Tears were forming in his eyes, along with no sorrow at all. Just plain weirdness tears, squeezed juice of rage. I slid back in with the girl. Lieutenant Johns paid for his Wrigley's Juicy Fruit and flints and departed. I was sure he had come to buy them in the Victory Luncheonette, not the PX, because he thought he might find me. The girl's knuckles were white on the edge of her Billie Holiday. She wanted to pick up her credentials and go elsewhere. Why hadn't I knocked him down? her knuckles were telling me. She had just finished conversing about how she was one-eighth Cherokee—or maybe one-sixteenth—it seemed to be a habit of adventurous southern girls. This Creole ancestor. This Indian chief, on her great-grandfather's side. Those were other liberal credentials—*but why didn't I knock him down?*

She didn't know about the Army.

"What happens to the Negroes, the colored people," I said, "it's totally unfair. Loaded on trucks. Engineers, you know. But there's one, he sings, he's an opera singer, they keep him at the Officers' Club. I talked to him when I was . . ."

White knuckles on Billie Holiday.

". . . assigned to clean up . . ."

She was searching for a sweet and well-brought-up North Carolina way to spring herself.

". . . clean up the, um, Officers' Club. This colored singer is a graduate of Juilliard, you know, the school in New York."

"Well, so long, I got to be toddling, so long, it's been really nice, thank you so much for the milk shake, I do indeed enjoy, really did, talking to you—"

I was alone.

Well, why didn't I just kill Lieutenant Johns? I could jump him from behind. I knew about knives, garroting, sudden, small-trajectory blows on the back of the neck. I was well trained, and he was pink and small, with breakable blood vessels. Why not?

But I didn't. I was still in the Army. The Army frowns upon the murder of officers outside of combat situations, and in my years as a soldier, I learned to accept some of this view. In my heart I objected to the Army way, but in my conditioned reflex, I accepted it. I was surviving, wasn't I?

Instead of grief over loss of the round-headed Billie Holiday scholar, I had boyish dreams of revenge against Lieutenant Johns—so naked of confidence was I. I dreamt of murder.

He wasn't finished with me. He ran a little corner of the meat machine at Fort Bragg in which enlisted men were ground up. We lived as separate from the disasters of old Europe as Lakewood, Ohio, is separate from Kamenetz-Podolsk.

A few days later he thought he caught me sleeping when I should have been on guard duty. I was curled up, head on my overcoat, hands between my knees in the dawn light, breathing softly, thinking. I don't know what I was thinking. "Soldier!" he bellowed. Sol-*ja!*

"Unh, unh," I said, removing my cramped hands from between my knees. Actually, it's hard to get comfortable on the packed earth in front of an armory. Actually, I was providing myself with the dream time characteristic of true poets like Morgan Delaney, George Sylvester Viereck, and me, and necessary to their mental health.

"Okay, soldier, you're up for court-martial."

"What?"

"Didn't you hear me? Straten up there!"

"Why?"

"Sleeping," he shrieked, "on guard duty!"

Me derelict before this armory in North Carolina? I wanted to ask, but he didn't want to answer. He seemed to think that sleeping on guard duty in time of war, even if all you really have in mind is gathering myth and memory into a great ball of genius, is punishable by death. Aw, no. Aw, gosh. I was marched off to the guardhouse.

The Army seemed to have a time-clock theory of work. The idea was not to do the job, but to do it within set limits of time. In real life, I tried to get my work done expeditiously. Standing guard, for example, I could do a grand job of eight hours of vigilance in, say, twenty minutes. After that, I just got drowsy.

As a result I was waiting for court-martial. I wanted to

explain how I concentrated my custodial talents and spent them in a mighty rush of intense and passionate guarding. The Service didn't understand.

Fortunately, there was a rush call for translators, and papers stating that I could learn languages fell out of a file. My court-martial papers never caught up with me. A clerk drank coffee on them or filed them. He had this whole long day for making mistakes. If you don't work so long, you don't have so much time for mistakes.

I was marching to the airfield to be shipped by fighter plane to learn to interrogate Russian prisoners captured with the Germans. Lieutenant Johns was strolling along the tulip bed near the general's house. He disliked finding me out of chains. His pink exasperation said: Where is justice in these degenerate times? Straten up, America!

My neck was swelling around the knot of my tie; I had dozed as I marched—another economical habit—and dreamed of revenge. Well, lots of time to dream. Someday, a network of fantasy linking everyone, I would surely meet him. And when the war was over, we would all be equal again. Maybe I could even look up the part-Cherokee North Carolina liberal. Who would nurse my bloodied fist back to health. After I beat Lieutenant Johns into clabber.

Camp Ritchie, the military intelligence post in Maryland which has since been reconstructed underground as a bide-a-wee home for the President in case of atomic attack, was then filled with language experts, creep-and-crawl freaks, Mitteleuropa refugees, heroes and young men fixing to be heroes. We rehearsed warfare in funny languages, using maps in Russian, Chinese, or Japanese to maneuver in Maryland apple orchards, finding Baptist country churches marked with the Russian symbol for *tserkov*. I was as ardent to train in these peculiar conditions as I had been to goof off under Lieutenant Johns' command. They called me *priki bobr,* the Russian for "eager beaver." In the company of other four-eyed goofs and *priki bobrs,* we crawled under machine-gun fire and learned to garrot, knife, and leap silently onto sentries, killing in our assigned languages.

On weekends I dreamed of finding a round-headed little lady who wished to be an apprentice hero's girl in Baltimore or Philadelphia, and somehow this time I did. Oh Lord, not another sex episode. She was separated from a chiropractor and planning her divorce; I turned out to be part of the plan. I won't explore all the ins and outs. We spent a weekend in the Ben Franklin Hotel in Philadelphia, where she taught me chiropractical things until my head spun.

Her name?

Forgotten. Remembered. Martha.

Oh, Martha, you were a tiger. Round head, hair bobbed short "for the duration," a little line of determination at the corners of mouth, pulling tight against the spongy area of early dissipation. More dark sponginess under the eyes. If you hadn't watched me so carefully to note the reactions of an innocent, Martha, you'd have been perfect. Curiosity was your big wartime emotion. Strange thoughts also flitted through my own brain, such as: Bet Lieutenant Johns never had a girl do something like this. Maybe a boy, but not a girl. I was vindictive, and even during that long weekend in bed, far from the reality of my nineteen years, close to the dream of my nineteen years, I was meditating revenge. It's bad to turn good sex into a means of getting back at someone else, a third party. I seemed to have some bad habits.

Martha shook her damp hair off her forehead and smiled at me. "What else would you like?"

"A milk shake? You like to go downstairs and get a milk shake?"

"No," she said, smiling. Tenderly she gazed into my famished face. "A Jewish person makes a good lover," she said.

"I'm a person, period."

"Nice boy, nice boy," she said soothingly. "What else haven't you ever tried?"

"How do you know what I have or haven't done?"

"I like you the way you are. You're fresh," she said. "Come on now, just put your head here, I won't hurt you."

And she didn't. I ached, but didn't hurt.

Since this was true love, not just a weekend flop in a hotel, we corresponded ardently, though it turned out that we couldn't meet very often, due to the war and her finding someone in her husband's chiropractic society and they had a lot of bonecracking in common. She was gentle. She replied to many of my letters. She was sweet. She answered perhaps one in five of my letters. She was kind. She left me with memories.

She turned me back to poetry, a consolation in time of war and requited, then re-unrequited love. I decided to become a published poet, and thus to make my mark on the world, to master my inchoate experience, to invent a better (and sometimes a worser) man to fill my own melancholy self, which remained a Private First Class after three years of shuttling about to be educated in various causes, from B-25 armament to the Russian language. I knew how to name the parts of airplanes in Russian, and I had been trained to recognize the rank of Soviet officers at a glance, and I even worked at interrogation of the black legion of General Vlasov, who had fought beside the Germans. But I wasn't sure who I was if I wasn't a poet and lover. So far, I was neither. Easiest to become a poet. I read Montaigne on self-knowledge: "His mind was so vagabond and his manner of living so diverse, neither he nor anyone else knew what kind of a man he was."

But I knew. I would find the truth. I began scribbling, and lo! in a few months I was a published poet, like Morgan Delaney. I sent out my verse without paying postage, due to service in the U.S. armed forces. I parachuted in a state of academic puzzlement when one of our team panicked at the stick, high above a southern meadow. I kicked him and followed, well-trained at last. He had reached the age of fear. I was the Jumping Interpreter, floating swiftly down behind enemy lines. It was a mistake to try to use old men of twenty-eight.

Roosevelt died, the atom bomb was dropped, my services were no longer required. While the bombs were unloaded on Japan, I was waiting in Camp Beale, California, to be shipped to China where I would at last see combat, providing liaison and translation between the U.S. Army and our gallant Soviet allies invading the Asiatic mainland. When two Japanese cities exploded, I thought: Well, I won't see China for a while. (I had also been studying Chinese, mainly Chinese map-reading.)

No-see-China. A fraction of a haiku.

No-see-Japan-either. A larger fraction.

Lined up for a solemn announcement, I had thought Roosevelt's death important. We weren't lined up for a solemn announcement about the atom bombs and knew nothing but that the war was ending. We sang in the showers afterwards. I would become a civilian poet, paying my own postage. I turned off my imagination of those two Japanese cities as I turned off the shower spigot. There was a lot of towel-snapping, American kids playing, American boys relieved at not having to make a tricky voyage to China.

I knew about the concentration camps. I always knew

about the murder of the Jews. It was peculiar after the war, when the camps were opened and the pictures of mounds of bones flooded out, that people said, "I didn't know." But I didn't know how different this bomb was.

All during that time of ignorance, I thought I had a mission to be a poet. I confused the fate of the Jews with the oath of revenge against Lieutenant Johns. To try to keep myself in order, I began to write about these things. I dreamed hatred, justice, sweetness, true love, and my past and future. I nurtured rage and anticipated murder. As the poems were published I felt twinges of satisfaction. But they were only twinges. Unease about my ignorance, which I knew to be without limits. Where to begin to end my ignorance? My poems didn't tell me that.

One day an editor wrote to me: "Seems you should be writing prose."

And I had a fresh revelation. Yes, not poetry, but stories.

I made a solemn vow. I went on writing poetry, but I didn't publish it. Now and then a love poem, occasionally a hate poem, but into the folder with them. Lieutenant Johns had a hard time at the hands of verse in those dying days of the war, when elsewhere the bodies lay piled like twigs, when invisible particles of bodies floated up into the ceaseless atmosphere.

I still believed that words in a notebook create the essential truth, a bond with history. The will of the midwestern boy to make art and love, find joy in his dream of it, was proud of its loneliness. Arrogant in isolation, I heard prayer as a banality and a mystification. I wondered if I even had a father and mother, so self-created did I think myself. I felt curiosity about the past, but it was an entertainment. I traveled through childhood as a magic spectator. I was willing to be amused and hurt, but nothing could really harm me. I was immortal. This was also the way to jump out of airplanes without fear. I landed on feet, knees, arms forward, tumbling, head tucked in, letting the weight continue the free fall, even on earth, and then arose from this dizzy flight as if from sleep, ready for combat. I would invent my own times, my duties and freedom, my America, my language. I was a child.

Now childhood was ending, along with the war I had in fact not invented, and I began to need actual others, family, a history that was not mere play, like Saturday afternoon at the movies or combat games. The traditional ceremonies of mourning and celebration became real. I, too, could die. I might also live.

TWO

5

In late spring of 1946 I was released, after three years, from the Army but not from literature. I spent a few months at home, decelerating and reading Proust. I arose each morning at reveille time, put on fatigues and boots, drank orange juice and coffee, made my bed as the Army had taught me, and marched off to my parents' attic to fight my way through the thickets of Swann, Guermantes, and the Baron de Charlus. In the afternoons I played tennis, and in the evening I hunted for girls but found mainly my high school buddies, also back from the war and spinning their wheels in the void.

"Gettin' any?"

"Some. Not much. No."

But I was getting some Proust, anyway. And suffering lascivious regrets concerning the chiropractor's wife. Lucille and Susan were part of the past, before the war, and Lakewood was finished for me, and besides, I didn't know how to find them.

The war was a rapid pivot for the sons of my generation. We spun round and round off family, shot out into strange places, and then many of us floated straight back to where we were. That can't be.

For example, take Stanley Strassberg, distinguished only son. He was a good boy, model airplanes, clean room, friendly to his mother, never complained about the braces on his teeth. He wanted to be an engineer, not a doctor, and his mother tolerated this foolishness. There was still time. He went through OCS and came to command a small island surrounded by a sea of kamikaze attacks. He fought in sand and jungle, received decorations, and survived. Then he returned to Cleveland, his mother, his room with all the model airplanes she had kept for him. "You'll wait till fall," his mother said. "Then you'll go to medical school. You'll live with us until you find a girl. Of course, who could be worthy of you?"

He didn't worry about that problem. He let himself be moved back into the room kept intact since age thirteen.

The war hero, a little tense and quiet, played with balsamwood toys. He made new airplanes with glue and string and a Woolworth's kit. His mother watched him shower to make sure he cleaned himself real good (glue on his hands at breakfast). She told my mother Stanley turned around so she shouldn't see when he dried himself with the towel. He didn't seem to remember all the good times they had when he was one and two and three years old.

The survivor from the Pacific cracked up under kamikaze attack by his mother. He swallowed glue, he choked as it tried to harden, he nearly died. An intern in the ambulance went into his neck with a pocket knife. A nice young Jewish doctor performed his first tracheotomy—*his* mother could be proud. Stanley was called a little nervous, jittery, a little schizophrenic; Stanley's mother wailed—it was due to the war. He was given drugs and shock. His neck healed, but he forgot how to eat. He weighed barely a hundred pounds. He was released.

Again he lived with his mother. He was very quiet. He drank warm milk. When I saw him with a cigaret, I wanted to tell him he was too young to smoke. He looked like a sick child smoking a cigaret. He wore a perpetual puzzled frown. I found him stroking a model airplane in his lap the last time I visited him. I didn't know him any more. Though we had been childhood friends, or at least our mothers had exchanged the news across Cleveland during the years of our childhood, the war and madness put the world and a universe between us. He didn't want to be an engineer any more. He didn't want to command a group any more. He went away again. I heard he was fed intravenously. He weighed eighty-eight pounds. His father pined. His mother was distressed. They tried everything, and when the money was gone, the Veterans Administration accepted the burden. He died.

Stanley's parents went to live in a dry climate. Tucson. His father didn't survive long. His mother is still alive, returning to Cleveland now and then to report on her longing for her son, the war hero. She is senile, but otherwise thrives in a dry climate.

I've begun about Murray with the extreme tale of Stanley. These were the Cleveland sons, the boys of my mother's friends, those examples of how to be nice. My mother wanted me to keep in touch with my own kind, and now that the war was over, I rewarded her for those prayers which had kept me alive. I also wanted to punch the last time clock on the job of childhood. I would have found Michael Fergus, too, if I could.

I found Murray in a difficult condition, a Cleveland son, a veteran, a Navy flier with good service. He had sensitive reflexes and a talent for music. His father, a CPA, had paid for violin lessons, but later he fell in love with the piano. The family had some money, they lived on a boulevard in Shaker Heights, and he, too, returned to the bosom.

At the time I was warring with family about my own future. "You'll be a doctor," my mother would say.

"No, a philosopher."

"Wah? A surgeon, a general practice, even a psychiatrist you like to talk so much."

"No, I don't want it."

"A surgeon, you'll learn how to cut. We'll pay."

"No, I get the GI Bill anyway. I think I'll do graduate work in philosophy."

She began to wail. I was a crazy.

My father listened and aimed to make peace. "You'll go into business with me," he said in his role as peace-maker. "Like that you can practice a little philosophy. You'd be surprised what a demand for philosophers we got in the real estate business. Also to be good with figures."

"No," I said.

"Oh, sure, why not?" my father asked.

"No."

"Yes you will. It makes sense."

"*No.*"

"Okay," he said, and turned to my mother. "You heard him, didn't you?"

"He's stubborn," she commented, as if to say, He doesn't realize he can give up this bad habit if he only tries.

"What can you do?" my father asked.

My parents gave up. The din quieted. There was dispute, and then there was peace, blessed peace. I didn't live at home; I left Cleveland; and I was forgiven. Occasionally, when things got busy in the real estate business, my father asked himself aloud why he hadn't held me out of the window by the ankles until I saw fit to do right, as some firm fathers did. Does the world need more critiques of Aristotle and Plato? The world needs someone to deliver brooms to the custodian at Euclid Towers. Other men had sons (he answered himself).

And I, too, wondered why I needed to go so far away to find home truths. (Home truths are not found at home.)

Now back to Murray Poston. He was spending the summer at his parents' one-acre ranch in Shaker Heights. His father had bought him a dozen ten-dollar postwar fabric-shortage silk neckties, $120.00 in ties in 1946. He could use the second car all he wanted—a Hudson. His father urged him to take it easy for the summer and then come into the accounting firm. After all, he was a handsome broad-shouldered Navy flier with certified reflexes and a possible Jap kill. He should be able to learn accounting at the top.

Murray, however, had this peculiar idea. He wanted to study the piano with Nadia Boulanger in Paris. He wanted to be a concert pianist. He played pretty well, not well enough, of course, but he was willing to work. And then after a while, he thought, drinking breakfast coffee in his fine Navy gabardines distractingly set off by a ten-dollar silk tie, he would compose like Bartok, like Schoenberg, like Murray Poston . . . He argued with his parents, sitting in gleaming modern kitchen chairs which were attached to their bottoms like prosthetic devices. He sat and argued in sumptuous red leather (the den). He made the mistake of trying to convince them, and therefore became a son again very quickly instead of remaining a Navy flying officer home on terminal leave, bearing sealed orders and command decisions. They listened to him pounding away at the piano they had bought when he was young, because it was nice, it filled up the room so nicely, and they thought: This is our son, who could go into accounting with his father? Who is trying to practice all the hours he missed during the war—who could be so good with figures? Who could be an auditor and eventually a CPA?

Who was now playing "Liebestraum" at midnight after he could have died in the war?

A rotten shame and terrible.

Rumor of the battle for Murray reached from his family's kitchen to my family's kitchen. A psychiatrist added to the picture, of course. Murray needed to unwind after cruel doings in the air of the South Pacific. Family scenes and tribulations. Since Murray was a strong broad-shouldered officer in the reserves, he would come out big, bushy-tailed, and boisterous (1946). Since we were prewar acquaintances and it seemed important to make old civilian life continuous with new civilian life, I telephoned to say nothing much. He said, rather coolly, "Drop over some night." As an enlisted man, I wasn't insulted. Only minimally cordial, but after all, he was a future student of Nadia Boulanger's in Paris.

It was a Cleveland summer evening, flies and mosquitoes and distant sounds of dance music on the radio in a maid's room. It was like summer vacation in high school, as if the years had simply been slipped out of our lives and the discrete pieces haphazardly fitted together, like war-surplus jeeps. We were not what we seemed, and yet we were only what we seemed, two boys home on vacation and eating a lot. Murray was ill at ease, too. He opened a bottle of beer and handed it to me. We sat on the rockers and swing of the back porch, looking out over the victory garden still tended by his parents. These prosperous people, ten-dollar neckties, maid, and cook, grew asparagus, corn, and tomatoes on their Shaker Heights rancho. The war had struck home. They discovered that they liked gardening.

"What you been doing?" he asked me.

"Nothing much, Murray. Looking around."

"I know how that is."

"You?"

"Same thing. Want some strawberries?"

His father was crazy about strawberries. He plucked the stems, sprinkled sugar over the rosy flesh, and left them to sweat their juices in a Pyrex bowl in the refrigerator. Murray spooned out two portions of strawberries, took two more bottles of beer—we were having beer and strawberries, it seemed—sighed, and returned to the porch. It was very hot, with a country stillness except for the insects. On Murray's base they used DDT to calm everything that flew which wasn't the U.S. Navy issue. We ate strawberries, drank beer, got sleepy, and had that late-forties, early-television conversation: "I don't know, Murray, what do you want to do?"

But then, *pow.*

In the middle of a nothing, Murray suddenly leapt up, threw a switch—the whole victory garden lit up in the dark —flung himself under the couch, came out with a rifle, and was firing away, *pow-pow-pow!* There was a fleecy leap. There were ghosts or kamikaze Migs or torpedoes in the garden.

"Murray! What the devil!" I yelled.

A rabbit lay bleeding and dead. Murray smiled. "Eat the vegetables," he said, panting a little.

A rabbit. Well, I knew about combat fatigue and the problems of a vegetable garden. I stilled my heart. Perhaps it was nearly rational, a semi-rational act. He switched off the floodlights which lit the yard. We went on talking. "Yeah," he said, "I practice three-four hours a day, Czerny, Chopin, Bach. The folks don't mind the noise too much, but my dad thinks—"

Lieutenant j.g. Murray Poston talking.

"My dad says—"

War hero Murray quoting his father.

"He wishes I would be the son he—"

"I know how that is. Me, too," I said.

"The business is growing, lots of new tax clients, only I'm really not interested in law or accounting."

"Well then, what I think—"

Pow! Flash of light! Murray at the railing! Rifle out and blazing! An eek and squeak and leap into the air! (Another dead bucktoothed rabbit.)

All these bloody interruptions. It was the piano he wanted, but the rabbits who died. The violence was rational, and yet not quite sensible. True, if they ate the plants, there would be none for the salad; but on the other hand, if he killed our conversation, there would be no conversation, either. The motive seemed a bit unclear. Stupid as I was at twenty-one and a half, fresh out of the Army, I knew enough to wonder why else he needed to shoot the rabbits. I knew why he shot the rabbits. Very simple—because it's a violent world, with terrible rivalries, and to keep them from eating the garden. Because he told me. And about the other reasons, I would drink the beer, eat the berries, and not ask him to explain.

Toward midnight I said, "Well" (dramatic sigh), "I guess I'd better."

Murray said, with a glance at the garden, dramatic yawn, "Me, too."

We shook hands very formally. God hadn't meant us to be close friends. I went to a bar where some terminal GI's like myself gathered to drink, and I drank with the fellows and exchanged the names of outfits and schemes for the future (sex, money, fame, power), not all of it clear over the pound of the jukebox. Transit time and transit noises.

• • •

Murray's father won. Murray is now just as good as a CPA. He gave up the piano. His children take, though. His wife is plump, with shiny pink hair. Murray is fat. He has had his first heart attack. The kids don't appreciate him. He has heavy legs, straining against his thighs. He likes to work in the garden. But he has been ordered to put no butter on his garden-grown vegetables and that is a deprivation for a boy who always liked to eat. Odd that his father is still alive, head of the firm, skinny and nervous and full of fight, when the son has to watch it so carefully.

Perhaps it isn't so bad for Murray. Stanley, on the other hand, is dead, leaving no child behind to ask, "Which war were you in, Dad?" His mother still lives in Tucson.

Nadia Boulanger, born in 1887, is retired and no longer teaches the Americans in Paris.

6

Something about living at home, something besides the absence of the chiropractor's wife, the presence of Murray and Stanley, was making me uncomfortable despite the nice peacetime coasting downhill. The hero was home and not to be disturbed. The hero headed for New York to continue his career as student of philosophy, poet emeritus, secret inscriber of stories. I took the train this time, a step up from Greyhound and Trailways, an abstention from boyish and soldierly hitchhiking. I slept in a Pullman car, lyrical as Thomas Wolfe and George S. Viereck, but discovered that the hypnotic clicking and churning of train wheels did not put me to sleep, as it does in stories. It made me imagine a slim poetess in my arms; okay, except that my arms were empty. I arrived tuckered out at Grand Central Station.

Almost at once a classical Manhattan fate overtook me. A lady who had read my poems in *Hex:* the review of Magic and Midnight, invited me to tea. What I had imagined on the long train winding across Pennsylvania seemed about to come true in Greenwich Village. She lived on soft and sooty West 11th Street, a near neighbor to the ghosts of Herman Melville, Henry James, and Edna St. Vincent Millay, and she was not only a lovely lady poet with a silent daughter who played in a dollhouse in her bedroom—a normal New York mystery— she was also a moneyed person who loved to aid and abet young poets. Mark Twain also lived in the neighborhood. Maxwell Bodenheim. e. e. cummings.

Due to the hope of getting some flashy sexual exercise, I didn't mention that I had already retired from my poetic career. I suspected (intuition of a retired poet) that she was disappointed to find me so young—still like an adolescent, with a skin sensitive to chocolate chip cookies—and it would ring the death knell to erotic corruption with the Founding Patron of *Hex* if I admitted I was no longer submitting eulogies and elegies to magazines. She was interested in results. She wouldn't respect my private manila folder.

Her name was, say, Miss Sterling St.-Martin. She had prematurely gray hair, prematurely crinkled eyes, prematurely long teeth; but she was slender and lithe, with a soft little hand, and the heiress to all that was Edna St. Vincent Millay. She also had a daughter. Her daughter had been a brilliant child from the ages of two to two and a half, speaking entire sentences of wit and poetry, and many of them Miss St.-Martin had written in her notebook, so worthy had she found them in her quadruple role as mother, critic, poet, and patron of the arts, but since then, the kid had gone into some sort of literary decline, not even saying Mummy. Miss St.-Martin waved away toward the bedroom, pushing sadness from us as if it were cigaret smoke.

"Tea?" she asked.

I wondered if I should tell her about the fantastic recoveries of sick children I had known in Lakewood, the illnesses of my fellow veterans, the brilliant neuroses—fascism, arrogance, uxoriousness—of my Army buddy, the poet Morgan Delaney. Probably all in due course, when I sorted out my shyness. She had a bright and speculative gleam in her eye and I wondered why, and then I knew it was because she had asked me, "Tea?" and she thought I had been thinking about the answer all this time. Well, in a way. I had been thinking about answers. I had been thinking. I had been sunk into reveries of the past because the past was when I had dreamed this dream which was about to come true.

Rimbaud also flowered young. "Yes," I said.

At last. She sighed. "Sugar? Cream? Lemon?"

"Yes, yes, yes!" I cried.

Arrgh, she snarled, leaping into my lap immediately after putting the kettle on. The kettle was throbbing and rattling on the stove and Miss St.-Martin was doing the same on my lap. I had been disturbed by her ankle-length hostess gown. I was afraid it hid swollen ankles, piano legs; but no, she really was slender and lithe, just as she had reported in one of her poems about herself, and her hair had been grayed by the excesses of a passionate spirit, exactly as she wrote.

Love I make it because I write it
Love I die because I will it

"The child!" I asked.

"Doesn't know what the hell's going on," she mumbled, biting my neck.

"Thank God," I said, blessing her daughter's idiocy, wanting to correct that impression, not getting a chance, giving up on clear statements.

"Oh God, oh God, oh God," she cried, and I drew back hastily, wondering if I had offended. Her fit of rapture continued for ten or fifteen minutes without my participation in any vital way. It was like the cuckoo clock shooting its little birdies out of the works, parading brightly in honor of the passage of time. I stood apart. I was amazed.

"Thank you," she breathed hoarsely.

Then I got my tea with cream. I peeked into the bedroom, where the pretty daughter, dressed in a pinafore, peeked out of a window of the dollhouse and winked. She had been expecting me, it seemed, and crooked a finger. I was about to crawl in with her, like a grownup from Lakewood, Ohio, but her mother said, "No you don't. She gets vicious."

Miss St.-Martin, lovely in long skirt, pink cheeks, and gray hair, was also smiling and crooking a finger. I drank my tea. The dollhouse creaked in the next room.

Later, on the street, I breathed deeply of the dry autumn air of Greenwich Village and thought to myself: This is New York, this is the literary life, this is what it's supposed to be. I was Dick Whittington within the gates of the golden capital. Dreams come true in this Manhattan, and I was learning about nymphomania, the Progressive Party, and the map of the subway system. I would never tell Miss St.-Martin about my retirement from the public enactment of poetry, but someday, when I knew her much better, I might hazard greater intimacy by asking why she wore a hostess gown when she had such good legs, and then why she barely needed to touch the guy when she united herself with him, and finally, as the climax to straight talk, I would confess that I was a poet emeritus, a writer of prose.

With a troubled spirit, of course. My soul would never know rest until I took revenge on those who had wronged me. Holy paranoia was not stilled by electric sex across a room with a defective child playing in her nest of blankies next door. It was as if I had communicated with Miss St.-Martin by whispering hot somethings into a telephone made of coffee cans and vibrating buttons linked by dental floss.

I struggled to keep my grip on a rage which was slipping away in a place where everything was exciting, everyone alert—how could I hate? I was healthy, doing all right. My memory of the Army was vivid, but fading—how I played Huckleberry Cohen to Morgan Delaney's Percy B. Shelley. My spite was fading, but vivid—how I played Benedict Foureyes to Lieutenant Johns, the Crule Avenger, with allergies, from the River Charles. I struggled to keep in touch with all the past I had, Susan, Lucille, the chiropractor's lovely wife, my family in Cleveland, the laden summer smells of Lakewood, that wandering year which was mine, the recent war which seemed the absurd dream of others, my childhood which had slipped like a set of toy cards through my fingers. Ferdinand Klabber, who was he? (My mother wrote that he now sold stamps in the Colonial Arcade.) Michael Fergus, where was he? (My mother wrote nothing.) There was a richer past someplace than the one I knew. My father was silent about it. He was a Jew, I was something. I longed to be continuous. Being told I was a member was not enough, no matter who told me. Even my class at Columbia College had been scattered by the war.

The society of literature might give me an allegiance, my fellow angels of the word, searching for truth and beauty and good sex, a good gang of fellows and girls, but I was caught between getting term papers in on time and a suspicion that even I couldn't be so stupid. No. Literature is not a nation or a religion.

Still, the city of New York, in the early springtime of civilian life, was a marvelous playground. I was released not only from the Army, but also from Cleveland. Undisciplined crowds liberated me. I kissed dogs, and sometimes their owners. Not even the chiropractor's wife was more profligate with marvels than the streets of New York.

One afternoon I was walking with my friend Grover Schuster down Broadway near Columbia during the first civilian Indian summer of 1946. We both wore our GI castoff pants, shirts, and boots, pleasantly aware of the fact than no one was bothering us to wear the hats. My war had been an easy one, my worst battles with the Army itself. Grover had been a scout for a platoon wiped out in the Bulge. He survived unhurt except for his nightmares, and after a time in a military psych ward, was studying law again at Columbia, trying to be a well-brought-up lad.

Already new hatreds were growing nicely in the fertile ground of the cold war. Street-corner barrages of sound-trucks serenaded us; this was Progressive Party, American Labor, Vito Marcantonio country. At 110th and Broadway the crowd watched a hoarse, bespectacled revolutionary in a khaki Eisenhower jacket over a blue workshirt pumping ideological air from the lip of a pickup truck. A delivery van stopped, a man leaned out and screeched at the speaker,

"Kaiiiik!"—a shrill jungle bark: "Kike kike kike!" He might have gone on practicing this crazed yell, except that Grover was climbing up the tire, over the hood, into the window of the van to pull him out. He came tumbling through the door with Grover, but he was dragging a wrench. The tool looked like a cretinous doll, with grinning steel jaws for biting. In a moment Grover's brains would be spattered. I thumped against the protruding running board of the truck, and as I came up, Grover was knocking the man's head against the door. The wrench fell on my foot. The man fell to the street.

We both then ran.

When we stopped, Grover was shivering as if with malaria, and he had a yellowish color, and I could see him again in his purple Army bathrobe, quaking with nightmares and drugs and the need to dream it out and out and out.

I talked him down. I told him my big toe hurt. Later I walked with a hole cut in my shoe. No wounds from parachute jumping and murder drills of all sorts, but now, as a civilian, I kept hurting myself. The wrench cracked a bone I had never before bothered with.

A thought about the truck driver gradually calmed both Grover and me: we weren't going to let him get away with it. I told Grover about Lieutenant Johns. I was sure to meet him again someday.

During these times I was spending midnights and mornings writing stories. The first ones were messy, and so were the later ones. Heavy purposes. They were about problems; they were about men who cried out in the night. I tried prying the lid off conventional memory. I wrote a fantasy about a middle-aged lawyer in Lakewood, Ohio, bored with his wife and family, who returned to playing children's games with the kids on the block. He came to no good end.

I sent it to one of the few popular magazines which was

reputed to publish "literary" stories. My general idea was to tell the truth. My general idea was to illuminate reality with a deathray blast of light. My general idea was to get some money to lift me out of my Amsterdam Avenue basement, and also to get some fame and love—a general idea not unlike the general idea of thousands of other young writers. Also, I sought to live in a reality more dense and vivid than my career as a GI Bill student from Cleveland.

Instead of getting the story back in the mail, I received a small envelope containing a thick rag of stationery typed on by a pale blue ribbon. The editor liked my story. She would give me money for it, two hundred and fifty dollars. She would print it in the magazine. But first, since she didn't recall seeing my name before, she would like to meet me, if this would not be too inconvenient, since I lived in New York, anyway.

When she saw that I was twenty-two and a college student, would she hate me? Or would she fall into confusing raptures, like the hostess-gowned poetess? To make sure of the address, I carried her letter down the narrow cavern of Madison Avenue. I stroked it like a talisman. I felt power all around me, the buildings swaying, my head aghast with dreaming, coffee alertness bursting in my ears. I was crazy with delight; I was terrified. There was vibrant purpose in all the bodies heaving themselves through the canyon. I was entering that radio drama to which I had listened on Sunday nights in the house on Hathaway Avenue in Lakewood— *Grand Central Station!* I was Mr. First-Nighter. My postwar suit, which I had bought at Howard's for twenty-one dollars, didn't seem adequate to the occasion, but I trusted my burning eyes to draw attention from seams and cut.

I'll call the magazine The Gentle Lady.

I'll call the editrix Miss Anabelle Loop.

I'll call myself Herbert Gold.

There I was in front of the elevator, pressing the button. Her assistant came to greet me. "Oh, Mr. Gold, how nice, how lovely! We adore your story!"

How nice and lovely this lady looked. Someplace deep inside I perceived that she had heavy legs, overly dimpled arms, a few moles more than normally required as beauty marks, hair defeated by steam heat, but her taste! her enthusiasm! her judgment of literature! She was adorable. This assistant editor's name was Sara. On the spot I resolved to write only great literature in order to live up to her trust in me.

Miss Anabelle Loop pressed my hand warmly and continued to hold it damply. She had discovered two great young writers that year; I was the second. She had surpassed her quota. She was filled with joy to make my acquaintance. They were looking forward to publishing my story in an early number.

There was one problem, however.

There were no Jews in my story.

"Of course not," I said. "I was, uh, raised in Lakewood, and my life in Ohio—"

"*Bien sûr,*" she said crisply. "That's fine. But your name . . ."

???

"We see no reason for your name."

"But that's my name, Miss Loop."

Long silence. Clacking of typewriters and heels in other offices.

"Does it *have* to be?" she inquired at last.

It turned out that the magazine didn't really like to publish Jewish writers in those antique times of 1946. And she had this neat idea, which can be summed up in one letter: "u."

By inserting a "u" between the "o" and the "l," I would magically become someone else, a person better and truer to my inner nature, to my story, and to the needs of literature; to wit, Herbert Gould. This midwife to the muse of prose explained how my career might be launched without distressing ambiguity, and since I was from Lakewood, anyway, and didn't speak with a hard "t" or a glottal stop or a ringing final "g," I might as well have a "u" in my surname. Herbert Gould. A new and more valid essence.

She wasn't delivering an ultimatum.

Only giving friendly advice.

In any case, of course, whatever I decided, entirely up to me, in the fullness of time they would print my story.

But could I think it over, please, Herbert? Herbert Gould?

I didn't have to think it over. "Yes," said sage Herbert Gould, "that's close enough. What difference does it make? Sure. Why not? Yes."

"You will never live to regret this," she said. "I'm sorry if the whole question is a bit *genante. Mille fois merci.* And I hope we have a new story from you very, very soon."

The beautiful Sara saw me to the elevator and pressed the button. I think that's the first time anyone pressed my elevator button. It was going down, and down I went.

Didn't sleep at all that night.

Didn't sleep that dawn, either.

Remembered my naked forearms in North Carolina, and the round-headed little Billie Holiday fan, and Lieutenant Johns telling me who I must be—just a good soldier and nothing more.

Called Miss Anabelle Loop the next morning, thank God it wasn't Saturday, and blurted out: "Herbert Gold. *Gold.* My father's name. Without the 'u,' please."

"Oh, that's perfectly all right, I understand absolutely, *complètement,* please don't be distrait," she said.

I sighed. Everyone was so nice in the publishing business. They didn't mind when I took to making difficulties and they were angels, *angélique.*

Whether to be or not a Jew, announced as that entity to the world, was a crucial turning in the road. I had come to this place without the "u" in my name. I may not have been a believing good Jew, but I was committing myself to my father, my brothers, and my unknown cousins everywhere; to trouble if necessary, to the meaning of the past, no matter how ignorant I might remain of it. I could be ignorant of it, but not a foreigner to it. Accepting this small part of my fate, I would take the rest as it came along.

Vanity and ambition tempted me another way. They might have put me to sleep with the dreamy ease of that "u." But the beginning of who I was could be told by a negative: *not to deny.*

A Jew. No "u."

When my story appeared, it was published back among the lingerie advertisements, in very small type, and it was unlisted in the table of contents.

Despite small setbacks, postwar life looked cheerful. There was a girl I liked, and another one, and then another, and I was busy getting degrees and getting published, even though I wasn't in the table of contents, and I was taking on a full consignment of civilian occupations. I was reading philosophy. I planned to be a deep thinker. I was writing poetry for my secret file and stories for the public one. A friend wrote to me: "Now you've broken through! You've done it this time!" I was happy for approval. I doubted that I had really broken all the way through to eternal truth and beauty, but I was willing for my friends to say so. At certain hours of the day I might think so myself. A magazine offered to print the breakthrough.

I had earned the right to get drunk in Greenwich Village with my fellow writers. We all heard of Dylan Thomas and how he drank at the San Remo, at the corner of Bleecker and Macdougal streets. Wine and spaghetti were my ideas of rollicking excess, and here I was taking rollicking excess with a real writer, Sam McGraw, who treated me like an equal although I was only twenty-two. He loved showing me the Village, where he lived, and talking about "us young writers," though I had the rude reflex of glancing at his bald spot when he used the word "youngwriter."

"I wish you wouldn't do that," he said.

"I'm sorry."

"I've crossed the middle of the journey of our life," he said, quoting Dante and Lionel Trilling.

"You're not even as old," I said, "as Christ when he was crucified or Herman Melville when he wrote *Moby Dick*."

"Thanks for that," he said. "But I'm getting thin up top, a little virile baldness, my doctor calls it. But I feel young anyway, though I'm nearly thirty."

He was thirty-one.

"I'm twenty-two," I said.

Our friendship wouldn't endure unless we changed the subject. He was my successful writer friend and I treasured him. All my other geniuses were unpublished and budding. I liked being in touch with a true professional, genius or not. "Let's walk up to the bookshop," I said.

Fateful stroll.

On Eighth Street a familiar small pink creature moved toward us, encased in a new floppy layer of flesh, but the original person lay nicely insulated inside, smiling and waving and saying hi from far away, saying hi from nearby, saying hi right next to me: Lieutenant Richard Johns, U. S. Air Force Reserve, Ret. "Hi and how are you!" he cried. "Long time no see! Whatcha doin' with yourself? Funny coincidence department, isn't it? Man, I met another guy just last week! Small World Department, eh? Personally, I'm with Merrill Lynch, investment advising on small accounts, that's what I'm doing, how about you? Looks like you went back to school, did I guess right?"

For it was indeed he. A flood of warming and stroking language which I recall thus approximately. No *rool* and *rat away:* the accent had changed again; but it was the same person.

Now remember my vows, remember your own vows. Remember my paranoia, remember your own. I had sworn to my nervous system (it was a means to survive) that I would knock him down. I had run the movie between my ears on numerous barracks occasions, consoling myself with bodily harm to my enemy. In my dreams I had destroyed him with fists and kicks so many times that this moment seemed redundant, and yet I was not crazy, I knew the difference between dream and reality.

In my dream I had done and sworn to do it again.

Now was my chance to do it once and forever and stop dreaming.

"That's right," I said, "I'm in school."

"Nice! Neat! Remember the Square myself, buddy. I was in Adams House. Wanna drink? Come on, old buddy, I'm buying."

Brainflash: the ice cream shop where he had robbed me of a girl without even wanting her for himself.

He was fat. He wore contact lenses, little shiny pimples on

the eyeballs in the glare of the streetlamp, a glassy two-eyed look worse than his former glassy four-eyed one. I took my own glasses off and put them in my pocket. Didn't want to break glasses when he hit me back.

"Hey, you know about Will Wright's? They got—don't I remember you didn't drink?—they got these great new flavors of ice cream! Bring your friend! Hell, how often you see old buddies from the Service?"

Sam was introducing himself. Being a writer, he didn't mind getting bought a drink or ice cream by a third party.

"Jeez, it's good to see you. Come on!" sang Dick Johns. "Rool out the bar-rel..."

I was trying to remember something. I must have looked funnily puzzled, standing there on Eighth Street near Sixth Avenue. At age twenty-two I struggled to recall hot rage and the cold desire to murder. I had treasured my grievance, and now it came to the moment.

I sighed. That was another life. It's hard to be strictly loyal to the past. I saw myself saying, *Oh, by the way,* and his surprised face as I guided his chin to my fist, and the disturbed waves of air as the mighty missile of my hate swept through the motes and the currents of Eighth Street, and a squish and sag as the man fell—

"Got to be going," I said, "got someplace we got to be. See you, okay?"

His face pink and sad, plumply working: here he found another old buddy who wouldn't let memories of the happy past ripen into friendship.

7

I had had too much Army, too many years as a boy, for dormitory life on Morningside Heights. Where I lived as a future husband was then an old-law slum with the Irish old-timers battling the Spanish new-timers in the center of tumbled New York. Out here in the real world, Amsterdam, Columbus, 103rd Street, there was rubble, like bombed-out London, where Rose and Garcia and certain odd old men, like George Sylvester Viereck, found rooms or flats. Mr. Viereck thought himself the natural son of the Kaiser and had got himself put in prison for Germany during two wars, a generation apart. To pass the idle hours between wars he had written the magical histories of my adolescence, those legends about the Wandering Jew and his secret of unendurable pleasure indefinitely prolonged. Now he was free again. I admired him from a distance; I never dared speak to my favorite Nazi. I watched him hobble sideways on our block, struggling home from the bodega, through confusion and arthritis, with his paper bags of groceries.

The block no longer exists. It was torn down for a project. Now it is "middle-income housing," a poultice on the wounds of the West Side.

"Don't let him do it to you, honey!" the old whore screeched at the ladies I brought home from the Graduate Libraries at Columbia. We would be discussing Weber and

Santayana and she would run out, poking her umbrella at us: "He'll try to get in your pants, honey, don't let him!"

"It's a popular neighborhood, popular in the sense of people," one little guitar-playing Progressive Party volunteer remarked.

"Don't let him lick you all over!" came the dying wail.

Columbus and Amsterdam avenues were parts of the old city in 1947. The Shamrock Bar and the Bodega-Carniceria dwelled side by side, like Jews and Arabs, doing business and quarreling. I was a student of philosophy, breakfasted on yoghurt and raw eggs, cooked kasha on a stove without a vent, and drank beer at the West End on the way home from Columbia afternoons, or during the evenings when there was no philosophic or progressive lady to be warned against me. The custodian greeted me by the number of my room, "Good e-ven-ing, Feefty-two."

Happy days of GI Bill Bohemia, sliding safely into civilian adult life. But there were also isolations and melancholias. *Who am I? what am I?* asked myself of myself in the delayed adolescence of the veteran's decline. And in partial answer it wasn't long before a graceful small lady came to live with me. I thought this would deal with the question, being a good imitation of adult life.

Then she asked her own reasonable questions. This was the winter of 1947–48 and she had a certain stubbornness: "Um, my mother wants to know where I live. Um, my mother is coming to New York to visit me. Um, where do I take my mother when she wants to see my room?"

Would it do for me to move out for a few days?

No, it would not do.

But I mumbled nothing that made the clear sense she sought. She did not press. The question hung there over the illegal stove which we had installed so that she could cook for me, like a good wife, though neither she nor the stove was legally vented. It was a room for one. Her mother was on her way any week now. I wasn't sure I should get married just because of the housing shortage and the visit of her mother, but these were considerations anyway, which, according to the Vienna School of Logical Positivism, as adumbrated in Chicago, at the New School, and elsewhere, meant they had to be considered.

"I should write my master's essay," I uttered aloud to the ceiling, the stove, and anybody who happened to be listening. "I got lots of work to do."

"Who's stopping you? In fact, I can type," said the lithe and lovely person who happened to be resting by my side on a Sunday morning.

"First let's read the *Times*," I said.

And wondered why I wasn't living alone once more, with the screeching old lady watching out for the virtue of my visitors. And the gallant custodian bowing and grinning and smiling. "Meester Feefty-two, good e-ven-ing!" And just pumpernickel and cream cheese for breakfast, stoking up the mental furnace of a man writing his essay on "Truth and Beauty in Plato and Hart Crane." (Hart Crane was also from Cleveland.)

José was my friend, but the landlord, who charged according to free-market principles for the converted coal cellar named Feefty-two, was my enemy. When I complained about the rent, he expressed sympathy and had a bright idea: sue him. I had cut my hand opening a broken door. I was interested in lower rent, not a release from the insurance company, but he appeared one morning with a lumpy smile on his loafy face, one of those faces of the bread salesman who eats too much on the route, his Khrushchev legs planted far apart on the loose board which was the entry to my coalbin, and in his hands, a piece of paper to sign and a check for fifty dollars folded neatly between pinkie ring and adjacent plump finger.

"What's that?" I asked. It was the laughing man at the Fun House, but why was he hee-hawing so, rocking on the loose board?

"Your finger," he said.

"My finger?"

He winked. "Your finger don't need to ask, I answer anyways. Don't want you suing me, blood poisoning"—another wink—"gangrene, amputation. Here, take."

I took. I still have the little scar. The finger is swollen at the knuckle, a possible source of trouble. It limits my marriages to women who don't demand a wedding band on the husband's finger.

I cashed the check, but saw no reason there in my Progressive Party, Vito Marcantonio days not to continue organizing my fellow tenants to protest our rent. The landlord had promised a garbage-disposal chute, cleaned-up hallways, improvements in the electricity, such as noninflammable wiring, and with those promises, together with some cash neatly folded between pinkie ring and palm and offered along with the handshake, he had been awarded rents by the city rent-control office which we, righteous and angry tenants, found unjustified. We hired a lawyer. Sandy hair, the washed-out blue eyes of a loser. The landlord came to my door as usual, collecting the rent, and said, "I gave you fifty dollars which you didn't even think you were entitled. When you wanted a place to come in off the rain, I gave you an umbrella over your heads. You're living here with a nice girl which I happen to know you're not even married. Okay, I understand these other people, okay, the Irishers, the Spanishers, but *you*—"

"I feel just like them, Mr. Ashberry."

"Ashenberry," he said gloomily, "not that it's my real name either. What do you mean you feel just like them? You feel, but you're not. How can you say that, a nice student from Columbia?"

"You shouldn't have raised the rent."

"All right, all right. Suppose we have a secret, just you and me. Suppose I give you a little personal rebate, say—"

"No."

"It ain't a kickback or nothing like that. It's just a little rebate between friends."

"No."

"You're meshuggah. I'll give it to you for Community Relations."

"No."

He sighed. "I have a son just like you, only he's at CCNY. He don't have all the advantages, like you. Columbia, I couldn't afford."

"I'm on the GI Bill. I can't afford your rent, Mr. Ashenberry."

Gloomily his midmorning snack repeated itself. He covered his mouth too late. Banana. "He's a good boy, just like you, only he got no respect, either. Look, you think you got a chance with this rent thing? What difference does it make in the long rent, Herbert? Long run, I mean, what difference? I get confused when I'm talking about my son, too."

I knocked at all the doors in the building to try to get them to contribute for our lawyer. The highest, furthest room was forty-eight, Gonzales. Feefty-two, the next number, was my half-basement bin. Some gave me five or ten dollars, some gave me promises, some refused to answer the door. Getting to know the People. One man, a functionary in a political party he refused to name, offered me a Chinese scroll, worth possibly thousands, as his share of the legal expenses. Getting to Know the West Side of Manhattan. Now I'm a Leader of Men, I thought; at last.

The day of the hearing arrived. Our lawyer asked all tenants to appear. A huddled and fearful little group followed him into chambers. The Leader of Men had the litigious flutter in the stomach: a sinking slide of gland and gut, a heavy wash of sour juices, desires to murder making omelets with desires to flee, all folded and simmering against each other in a delicate place directly below the belt buckle. Mr. Ashenberry wanted to shake my hand in front of everybody. "Listen," he asked, "does your dad know what you're doing?"

I took his hand because I didn't know how not to, but said nothing. He stood waggling his head.

His own son also had no respect.

"Is everybody present?" asked the judge. "Hey, no murmuring from you people back there"—he meant us—"or else we'll clear this courtroom. Okay, proceed."

Our lawyer was a well-meaning incompetent; Mr. Ashenberry's lawyer was an ill-meaning competent; the judge knew where the power belonged; we had our brief, tarnished moment in court and were back on the street. Our muddled lawyer, Sandy Loser (not his real name), ran for the subway as if it were the last train to leave lower Manhattan. Mr. Ashenberry did not gloat. "I tried to put an umbrella over your head when you needed an umbrella," he said, "and this is the trouble you gave me. Well, no hard feelings," and he put out his hand again. That man loved to shake hands.

I gave him my fifty-dollar finger along with the four others and he squeezed them for me. This was politics and race and something to talk about in bed. The war was over; real life had begun; injustice gave me a stomach ache. I returned the

Chinese scroll to the political functionary. I never collected the money from Forty-seven, Thirty-four, and other colleagues in the rent suit. Thirty-seven said to me, "Hey, why I paid, they didn't?"

"Do you want your money back?" I asked.

"Naw, never mind. Dirty deal."

It was my fault for losing. It's better to win. My belly hurt.

From the fire escape I saw Mr. Viereck, my childhood hero. He moved very slowly. The effort of walking with his groceries made his lower lip tremble. When someone bumped his leg, the powdered puddings tumbled out. Junket, Jell-o, Tapioca. By the time I got down to the sidewalk, he had picked them up himself. He too must have had difficult innards, due to two wars wasted in American prisons.

One day I had a stomach ache and it seemed to be more than metaphysical indecision or too much kasha. I went to the college infirmary, where they took my temperature and said not to worry.

The next day it was worse and an intern asked me, "Do you normally complain a lot?"

The next day my appendix burst and I lay cut open, limp, and tube-infested in the Bronx Veterans Hospital. During my brief spells awake, my roommate tried to convince me of the virgin birth. "You ketch diseases from a germ! Sperm is a germ! Why couldn't you catch a sperm germ from the air?" But the morphine made me sleep a lot. Waking, I couldn't say why not before I drifted off again.

A dim insistent voice kept buzzing at me through morphine: "Jews accept the germ theory. Pasteur. Why can't they accept the sperm-germ theory, Jesus Christ?"

During the month I lay in the hospital, toe-wiggling therapy by GI therapists-in-training, immaculate conception lessons by my colleague in the next bed, I also took visits from

Red Cross, USO, and Big Brothers, just as if I were still in uniform. The lady with whom I had been living came to comfort me daily. Sometimes she moved the tubes and dripping jars and climbed onto the bed. The sperm-germ man never complained, but she pulled the curtain so as not to distract him. Nurses, orderlies, and chaplains passed by without comment, but once the chewing gum and cigaret lady from the USO surprised the lady on my bed and said, "Eek." I agreed.

Finally they sent me home and she didn't have to make the long haul up a steel Veterans Administration war-surplus hospital bed. She had stored up some kind of erotic credit. Her mother was again imminent. Now that I was well, I should begin to reckon with facts. But I was still a weak man. My stitches were raw. I wasn't well yet.

One of my philosophy professors, Dr. Gutman, visited the convalescent in our tenement. He found time to care for a specific student in the abstract unease of Manhattan. He didn't come bearing a tray of gum and cigarets; he came direct from real life. Plato. Aristotle. Whitehead. The worth of the humanities. He sat by my bed and we talked about secretaries, jobs, fellowships, academic gossip to whet my appetite for hurrying out of quarantine, back to the graduate school playground. Cambridge. Oxford. All English philosophers stammer. While he talked, a siren drew nigh. As he continued talking, a ladder was thrown against the outer wall. I could see the mechanized stilts. Listening to his confidences about the chairman of the department, I noticed a fireman breaking my half-basement window with his ax. The blade of a hatchet sliced through plaster. A filmy halo drifted about the cockscomb head of another fireman. St. Louis Hegelians. Chicago positivists. Irwin Edman on Sunday morning. The fireman burst into the room, shouting, "Out, out, goddammit, everybody out!"

As he prodded us with his ax handle, Professor Gutman was saying, "My wife thinks we should spend the year in Paris, she doesn't care about the rationing, but London is where the Wittgenstein papers—"

A few little tongues of fire licked at a few little windows. Room Thirty-seven. Room Forty-seven. Nothing much. But the building was flooded. Mr. Ashenberry was wringing his hands in the street and crying, "Some more water over there! Not so much over here!" A maestro directing the full orchestra.

A few days later we moved back into the smell of damp char. Small gray tendrils of fungus visited on my window sill, feeding on the sinewy rubber moldings. There was a garden of furry lower life flourishing in the closet. My lady and I wiped, but found that keeping our minds on higher matters was a more lasting consolation. Mr. Ashenberry had put an umbrella over my head, but it was more like a lacy parachute as I tumbled down through real life in postwar Manhattan.

Despite my running into the street with the fireman, Dr. Gutman, and the lady, my stitches didn't break. Therefore back to the world of ideas. Seminar time again; three-by-five-card time.

Busy with philosophy, healing innards, and the ominous future visit to New York by the mother of the lady I had somehow taken to living with, I hardly noticed the convulsion taking place in Palestine. That was mere world news, and besides, I was an internationalist. I did not believe in national states. I believed in brotherhood. I believed Jews were the brothers of everyone, even if everyone was not brother to the Jews. I was an American of the Mosaic persuasion. I had had enough trouble with being Jewish to be addicted to my troubles and to insist on them. My father had chosen a name and I was a part of him. I would be what my name told others about me. But I saw no reason for a Jewish state in the Middle East, a little Lebanon or Switzerland or Haiti. The Stern Group had blown up the King David Hotel, and that was bad. The Irgun had made reprisals against the British, and that was bad. Some American Jews were screeching about a new state, and that was annoying. I had seen enough of women's clubs and professional Jews in Cleveland. I was busy waiting for my non-mother-in-law from Detroit.

In the springtime of 1948 I lived in a day-by-day fog of waiting. I was waiting to be not married. I was waiting to be freed. I was hoping to give the lady what she wanted, but since there was no other apartment available, and she was pretty and lively, and her mother was due any second, what else was a fellow to do? There was energy in the air. It wasn't my own, but it was becoming my own. The years of the Army had carved a hollow place in my life. It had interrupted adolescence, and now I was continuing my childhood. I paid constant attention to myself. I'm not proud of that. I was a seventeen-year-old who had lived twenty-some years, and found himself burdened with fantasies, words, ambitions, and the beginnings of obligation. Emptiness too was mine. Many emptinesses and vanities. That was a weakness which eventually can lead to autobiography. I was trying to notice the world, and living in mere desire. I envied men who wept, those who died for causes. I recalled sacrifices and miracles and felt dizzy with longing. I began to read history, Michelet and Gibbon. When there was an eclipse of the sun, I hardly noticed. I had books to read. I was writing poetry. I think there was an eclipse, and I looked up through the haze, and then went back to my Quine on logic. I looked for magic eclipses in the medieval scholastics. I squinted up past the Amsterdam Avenue feet thronging by my half-basement window, and saw by the passing dark that there was an eclipse, and bent back to my Hugh of Saint Victor and Peter Lombard. (The fundamental idea of things has reality, not the actual example in our paltry lives; "eclipse" is real, but the eclipse on any given day is merely temporal, and therefore should not cause awe. Oh, nonsense.)

When a stomach hurt, I had accepted the intern's notion that it was my imagination. I lived so much in imagination that why not? I then lived under morphine, bemused by a painlessness which was almost joy, but later wanted to go back to studying. I wrote poems detonated by a word in Santayana's *Reason in Science*. I wrote philosophic essays incited by a sentence from Hart Crane's notebooks.

Once, however, when a sharp piece of New York grit flew into my eye, I went to the hospital. I couldn't ignore the mote when it began to draw blood and lymph. It was more real than the idea of it. Nor could I truly forget that the girl at my side had a parent who grieved to discover that we were living together with only the landlord's blessing.

What were these doldrums? My life was no longer in question. To be gun fodder had been a kind of link with reality. The war was over, with my energetic dreams still dreams; and the cold war was upon us, the dreams of others distant and chill. I was ancient for an adolescent, but years of soldiering had deposited me back in civilian life just where I had been four years ago. How little I learned from eighteen to twenty-two as one of America's fighting men. An atavistic organ gave me peritonitis, my atavistic brain gave me a master's degree, my loneliness gave me a roommate, our drifting together gave us friends—graduate students, handwriting analyst, a composer of songs for Nat "King" Cole, a Morning-side Heights Reichean, some Progressive Party guitarists, a personal friend of Vito Marcantonio, a Belgian medical student, and some midwesterners stranded like us at Columbia. A little bit of kleptomania and a lot of fret about money and a stoical acceptance of the conditions of New York. I was a future professor, presently scavenging. The Veterans Administration didn't support us in the style we wanted.

At the Scribner Bookshop on Fifth Avenue, I was caught stealing *The Place of Value in a World of Fact*, by Wolfgang Kohler. I also had my eye on a book by Piaget about the social structure of children's play groups. The detective snorted with indignation complicated by a head cold, and held my elbow tight through the store, and put his face too close to mine as he filled out the forms in a basement room. I was registered as a book maniac with the Fifth Avenue Merchants Association. My side hurt. The scar felt as if it were splitting open. Oh, no, and I was a veteran, too. I was a poor fellow whose girl friend's mother was coming to New York, where she would find her daughter betrayed by an ex-GI book thief. But the girl wouldn't move out; housing was short; somehow we wanted to stay together, the criminal and the lady.

Said the detective, snorting, "We could get you booted out of school."

"I know," I said.

How did I stay wrapped in angry adolescence after so many adult activities?—learning murder skills, languages, and why we fought. If I were expelled, she would have to find someone else.

"But we'll let you go this time." the detective said.

"Thank you."

"Is that all you can say? You're a veteran. You're a student at one of our fine colleges and universities."

"Thank you and I'm sorry."

"That's better." He stood shaking his head in his stuffy basement which served the dual purpose of dressing room for male clerks and interrogation chamber. He wasn't sure it was so much better, but he hated to make a big deal of it. I must have been a sallow creature with lower lip shaking. He didn't want to squash me.

I hurried east to the river, with ideas of walking over the edge of the world. I paused at the grill of black iron. My shame was exhausted short of suicide. A poet and philosopher who drowned himself before becoming a famous thinker was just a soggy mess in the East River, floating end over end on a level with packing-house reject meat. Instead, I stopped boosting books, and also fruitcakes, small cans of food, items of apparel. Like Kierkegaard, I took to poverty. That nice detective lowered my standard of living.

Back home under the umbrella provided at non-rent-controlled prices, my lady was brooding gloomily over a letter. I didn't have to ask. It was from her mother. I thought of warning her: Did she want to marry a thief? A cross-examined thief? Like Kierkegaard, a fatal bachelor? But alas, I knew the answer. I was redeemable with patience and the love of a good woman.

The next day, when my GI Bill check came, I decided to celebrate my new non-kleptomaniac career with dinner in a Hungarian restaurant on Broadway at 101st. Even Sören Kierkegaard, the Danish pessimist and wit, enjoyed a good wine now and then, just like Morgan Delaney's father, the international sophisticate. It was a warm evening in May and my stomach had stopped churning, my scar stopped hurting, after the climax of my criminal career. There was that West Side nerviness in the air—pizza, fried chicken, automobile exhaust, bus fumes, and a streaked gaiety of spring on the thin mugs of New Yorkers. The old jowly ones clustered on their benches down the dividing strip; the young ones thronged the walks. We ate goulash, I think, and many-folded pastries, like fine paper soaked overnight in honey, and we drank too much coffee. The world news of cannons and raids was exciting; the waiter had undimmed his face, lights shone in his eyes; and when he abused his customers, it was with joy.

When we emerged, they were dancing the hora in the streets of Manhattan. It was May 14, 1948. There were signs leaping about in the hands of kids, held up like long-legged circus acrobats: Habonim, Hashomair Hatzair, 92nd Street Zionist Youth; and I looked at the gawky, precarious banners and at these frantic New York Jews with my eyes cooled in Ohio. My lady's eyes had been cooled in Michigan. Thirsty watchers ate tinted Italian ices, dark sweating ladies stopped to stare at the dancing children, street kids suddenly wearing yarmulkes whooped and leapt into the crowd. West Side strangers to this madness gathered in groups to watch. The early editions were out with their headlines. A hot night, and President Truman had made up his mind. Haiti had voted. The lady and I watched, amazed. We were internationalists by principle. We didn't believe in establishing another little Middle Eastern nation. We thought peace meant one great Union Now—no more gallant little Belgiums, tense little Switzerlands, irate little Irelands. We were radical and progressive, not internationalists. We knew a personal friend of Vito Marcantonio. We believed in universal fraternity. I thought I saw George Sylvester Viereck in the crowd. We didn't like these chauvinistic New York types.

My heart was pounding.

The lady may have thought I wanted to go home to bed. I thought the same. The secret of unendurable pleasure not prolonged at all. That was what the founding of Israel meant to me, an excitement common enough for a slothful veteran. "Let's," she said, "let's dance." I pulled her by the hand and we ran to join the crowd. I didn't care about their funny little nowhere nation—someone had already made the joke about changing its name to Irving—but I loved to dance with Jews, having lived so long with the sense that Jews were only my father and mother, the six million murdered, and trouble for me. There were others, these wild and prideful dancing ones; and now I didn't care about Union Now, I wanted to join the others, those whose cousins lived in funny little unviable nations, Denmark, Chile, Morocco, and I was dancing. I was an American of the Mosaic persuasion and from Lakewood, Ohio; but the widening circles of kids stopped traffic, broke over cast-iron fences and formed again, danced and sang; and huge black eyes, flushed cheeks, and flying legs had brought me into the whirling mass of celebrants. I was not Sören Kierkegaard or Morgan Delaney's father, nor was meant to be. I danced, we danced, it had happened. Somehow I heard that Haiti was one of the first to vote for Israel in the United Nations—why Haiti? And the Soviet Union. And Harry S Truman. Why such strange friends, everybody their friend, everyone our friend now? I had a stomach ache and danced. I thought: No more appendix, no more book-stealing; and the Hungarian stomach ache disappeared under orders from my soul, and we danced, my lady and I, singing songs we didn't know, whirling in a circle we had never joined, internationalists by principle but dancing the creation of just another little Middle Eastern state, just as if it conformed to our principles, just because our hearts and souls happened to rejoice.

I didn't care if her mother discovered us or not. Let her mother stay in Detroit; it made no difference. At this moment we both loved the same thing, and therefore we loved each other.

"Will you marry me?"

"Yes," she said.

Girls with longish, roundish heads mysteriously charmed me. I thought it was the smile, walk, intelligence, grace, but it turns out to be the head. Other strengths later come into play—the soul, the *person*—but first the head. I married a lady with a round head, but not a long one, and forgot the girl with different strengths who made me shriek in a darkened room of the Ben Franklin Hotel in Philadelphia on a weekend of Army leave. I didn't quite forget her.

I saw myself as the Young Veteran Energy Disposal Company. I was searching the community of art—that was who I was and where I belonged. The spasm of sentiment about Israel passed like other spasms. What connection did it really make with my life? Girls with round heads, driven but shapely paragraphs abided when the destiny of a people turned into a mere newspaper serial melodrama. What a confused idea. I knew that men had allegiances and I wanted some. Still I was reluctant to seize the ones naturally offered me, family connections, kinships in history, and aimed to

carve my own out of the brotherhood of wine-drinkers, ca-
rousers, poetry-declaimers, exiles in lack of silence and borrowed cunning. Candle drippings on wine bottles and spaghetti drippings on red-checked tablecloths. I took arms for
the cause of fair Bohemia.

In my mind, anyway. In soberer fact, I was half of a couple
of young marrieds in school on Morningside Heights. My
disposition was a cheerful rather than a loving one, but it was
the best that nature and history had provided and I was not
yet ready to provide myself with a better one. Crucial events
floated in colloidal suspension.

Dwight David Eisenhower, inserted as president of Columbia University in order to prepare him for higher civilian
office, expressed disappointment that his new rank did not
permit him to see more of the fellas. He seemed to think it
was Culver Academy and wondered when the college boys
would march. We marched when they raised tuition,
marched in front of his house on Morningside Drive, and
with pounding hearts thought we had done a great deed:
marched, shouted, and waved banners. The GI Bill did not
cover the new fees. My dissertation advisor stopped making
myopic, knee-craving gropes at me because I had disappointed him deeply: first married, then an agitator. It was the
war which had changed me so, he sighed. He sent me a
philosophic poem about the embittering and hardening of a
sweet lad who had come to New York by Trailways bus from
Lakewood, Ohio. And asked one last time if he could show
me his favorite Turkish bath. He was wrong about many
things; for example, I got to New York by the Greyhound.

I ran around the track three times a week with a former
bombardier-navigator. We ran at dawn, hearing the chirp of
blood in our ears like the birds of various country posts. This
was Manhattan, on the hill just above Harlem.

I discussed St.-John of the Cross and the problem of religious versus secular life with Allen Ginsberg. We sat at the West End Bar and shouted at each other about crime, Rimbaud, Wilhelm Reich, and weeping saints on bloodied crosses, and swore never to meet again—our characters and causes too disparate—and met again devotedly.

I watched my wife walking toward me on campus, and thought: Well, she's pretty, she's smart, she has a nice walk, and I'm married to her. We were like incestuous brother and sister, not yet sure whether we liked or disliked each other, not yet blaming each other for any ill or evil in our lives.

I envied Morgan Delaney, who adored his wife, all his wives, cared only for them, each one of them in turn, and wanted to swallow his life wholly into theirs. I was looking for a community other than marriage, but believed that if I failed with this one, I could not succeed with the other, no right to claim it. Love begets love, and only love begets it; but the duty to love begets dry boredom, which begets anxiety, which begets the desire to destroy.

I wouldn't have won the Clear-Thinking Returned GI Prize. My head was crowded with words like "illusion," "need," "hero"—Nietzsche, Freud, Carlyle—and coziness was far from my idea. Yet in fact I was trying to make cozy when I required depth in love. There were worse casualties of the time, but I was one of them. It was the age of togetherness, tract houses, and the baby explosion, and although we lived in a Manhattan slum, our romance was dimmed by family intentions. Sometimes one of us sulked over a failure to share the housework. Sometimes the sulker gave up sulking and made toasted cheese sandwiches, followed by conjugal love. I tried to think it through: Like me, she's midwestern, Jewish, goes to school, and speaks languages. She sews. Good with her hands. She dances a little tensely, but she dances. Probably I'm not so loose myself. And when I touch her mouth, I'm touching the mouth I most want to be friendly.

Good friendship was not my best dream, but it was the highest possibility of the fix we had chosen. We were sharing a life in the new postwar Bohemia—there's that healthy but creative couple, confident yet not disgusting, serious not solemn, a pair of genuine laughing free spirits, honest, friendly, reliable . . . Marvelously tolerant of weaker souls than their own, even ardently admitting to flaw while somehow managing to be treated as the hope of Morningside Heights . . . There they are again, the two of them walking together down Riverside Drive and through life, making likable jokes while they search for the Truth—*a burden to everyone.*

Unknowing, obscurely fettered, I sought community in the memory of Hart Crane and Plato, Whitehead and Blake, Homer, Dostoevsky, and Kafka. And Rudolph Carnap, the logical positivist. And Ernest Nagel, the symbolic logician. I drifted through the vocabulary and disciplines of philosophy, looking to become wise because surely I was not. I felt hair prickle and skin crawl at simple lines and phrases—"vexed by a dream," said Shakespeare, and I was a child again, vexed by repetitive dreams I could barely remember, and by the memory of those dreams. I had doubts. I needed to find my history and its meaning, and to give myself something beyond idea and self. Instead, I just went from day to day, cheerful and fretful.

One night we were invited to Allen Ginsberg's cold-water flat on the far East Side, across Harlem. Allen understood about my wife. He had great resources of tolerance even then; but I was early married for a graduate student in those years, and the others in the rat-tracked rooms stared—a couple? a couple? a *couple?*—as we pushed the door aside and entered. Oh Lord, here they come, one husband, one wife, the spouses. There were mattresses, orange crates, and extension cord rootlets striving out into the hall for the nourishment of sockets. (Bohemian bulbs are hungry and must eat, Bohemian radios are thirsty and must drink.) Some of the men in the room were poets, also a recent profession of mine, and they stared from their safe Parnassus as if my new full-time occupation was husband. Oh, but I'm not, I'm not! I wanted to declare. I'm married, but all I am is not what you'd call a husband!

"Why do you talk so funny?" a furry plump little non-versifier asked me.

"I'm from Lakewood, Ohio," I said. "That's a suburb of Cleveland." I skated on Rocky River. I sat in trees, looking at Lake Erie. I longed for Susan Norton.

The poet bugged out his big brown eyes.

You can speak freely, tell your secrets. I won't pass them on to the other husbands.

"Moshe Pupick the All-American boy," the poet said.

I decided to destroy him with a look. He didn't melt or faint, so I tried words on this early hyperthyroid case: "You're Jack Armstrong," I said, "if Jack Armstrong used a dildo."

When disappointed, I sought to be abusive, like native New Yorkers. One thing I had trouble learning: the friendly street gaming of it under all the crowded rage. When I was abusive, I was really nasty—Dick Whittington studying Manhattan ways, which are not so simple as a shove and a curse.

"I'm beginning to get you," said the poet. "You make yourself clear. You're a cunt."

Allen threw his arm around both of us. "Come on, come on, come on, you're two of my dearest friends, come on now."

Passionately I wished to understand Manhattan.

Red wine and some healing herbs. We lay on mattresses. Everyone seemed to settle into ease. My wife was unhappy.

Her unhappiness was gradually transmitted to the young men lying about and waiting for something to happen. To be the lonely only lady was not her dream at that moment—not in this place carpeted with extension cords and empty Saltine boxes. Nor was it the young men's dream that she be the only lonely lady. She sat on a lurched, bitterly arthritic mohair couch with an Esso map of Africa tacked to the wall behind her. Allen was saying, "I'm going to Africa this summer. I'm really going this time."

"Where?" my wife asked.

"Like Rimbaud, I'm going. I might not come back. Africa is the cradle."

"Where? Where in Africa?" my wife asked.

"I'm going by freighter. I don't know what I'll do when I get there."

"Where, Allen?"

He seemed to be starting to point, but then his arm changed its mind and drew back and a glass of wine started on the long voyage to Africa, past my wife's shiny dark hair, smashing against a cluster of French colonies on the west coast, sending shards of glass and streaks of wine down Esso-modified Mercator projection and clean, well-brushed lady's hair. "There," he said, "that's where I'm going."

"Christ!" I said.

Young men on mattresses as still as a bas-relief. Someone giggled. Allen looked morose and pensive, not quite proud. My wife aimed a steady righteous ire straight into my heart, wanting me to hit him, but a fellow doesn't do this to an old friend, a fellow poet, given to mysticism and the wisdom of the body, who surely wouldn't strike back. I knew him: he would suffer my assault with the forbearance of Alyosha.

"We're going," I said, trying to make this sound masterful. It was not masterful.

Allen stood courtly at the door to bow us out. In the green plastered hall, vines of extension cords led out to the place where a light bulb had been removed and a dense nest of double-sockets had been planted. The revolution against Consolidated Edison was off to a slow start. Allen watched us down this sad corridor.

We quarreled that night, my wife and I. She hated my friends. A smell of red wine arose from her hair as her wrath mounted, and I wanted to love her, to bury my head in her red wine, to say Never mind, you're my only dearest friend; but instead I only promised never to inflict embarrassment upon her again. Another promise I didn't keep.

I also promised that we would go to Paris. We could agree about that. We needed a change and Paris was where changes took place. New friends, new civilizations, the wisdom of the Old World, plus romantic strolls in storied Montmartre. With her fluent French, she could lead me around like a mute man and, in her spare time, tell me about matrimony and its duties. I asked the Philosophy Department to mail me my certificate; I was a Master of Arts; and all Europe would be my teacher. Like Rastignac, I would stand in the Père Lachaise Cemetery and cry out to the City of Light, "It's between us now." Or, depending on the interpretation: "Henceforward there is war!" Or, if I learned well enough: *"À nous deux maintenant."*

A poem informed me that Paris is the Paradise of Misery and the Capital of Hope. I was ready, then. We needed a community of serious thinkers. Paris was where the existentialists and the cold war exiles were gathering. The recent war was real and the coffee-drinking serious and the wine better in Paris. We would not settle for the facile careering of our fellow graduate students, scattering to temporary housing in universities all over the country. Forward, into mysterious *Wanderjahre à deux.*

Our life was a thrilling series, and the title of the new volume was "Crazy Kids Cross the Ocean." My wife laughed. Later she said, "I think that would be nice. Can we afford it? What are we getting into?"

"Don't worry," I said, "I don't want you to worry about a thing."

On the *Niew Amsterdam* over, we met a pioneer psyche-delic couple, Charles and Wendy, he a painter, she a painter, we instant soulmates. They were itching to get away from Minneapolis. We were itching to get away, too. "You wouldn't believe the level of insight in Minneapolis," he said.

"It's so low," she said.

"New York is crude, too," I said.

"So is Detroit," my wife said.

"Not to mention Lakewood, Ohio, where I came from," I said.

"That's not Manhattan, Bronx, or Brooklyn?" Charles asked, eyelashes fending off the difficult idea.

I was accustomed to this problem and all it signified. "No, actually I'm from the midwest, like you," I said. "My wife, too."

"Oh, we didn't mean anything by that," Wendy said. "Actually we're all artists, aren't we?"

The Crazy Kids Meet Other Crazy Kids, I thought.

Charles looked at me slyly. "We, too, married young—"

"Married young," echoed his loyal wife.

"But we haven't sold out."

"—sold out," echo said.

We waited for details. They were cautious. They liked us,

but were not sure they fully trusted native New Yorkers. Later, a day later—friendship accelerates on ocean voyages —it turned out that they were experimenting with expanding their consciousness here in 1949. They fasted, they took seasickness pills, and then they went to bed with a bottle of champagne. Terrific results. They didn't reappear for a whole day on the North Atlantic while all we did was watch the squall and drink tea. Salt blew in our faces, my lips were swollen with impact of spray, and what the devil were Charles and Wendy up to? Mere seasickness?

When we saw them again, they looked gray, stunned, and goofy, and had joyous private smiles. "We're gonna eat for a day," Charles said.

"Fatten us up good," Wendy said.

"Then," said Charles, as if it were a complete sentence with subject, verb, and firm clauses.

"And then," Wendy said, as if this was all Charles had left out. They smiled upon us. We were friends. Ohio and Michigan are the midwest, too. We were chosen.

"Wanna join us next time?" Charles asked, "wanna?"

"We never did a foursome with Jewish kids," Wendy said. "We're not scared if you're not. Okay?"

We rode the boat train from Le Havre to Paris with our friends Charles and Wendy. They were innocent and grudgeless. They forgave us our rejection of the intersexual, interracial (as they put it) foursome in the shared rapture of our first taste of French bread, French butter, which we took together and interracially in the dining car on the war-battered road through Normandy. We soared, we saw peasants, we swore eternal friendship, we knew this was a really deep moment in our lives. "As an artist, a man has no other home in Europe save Paris." *Ecce homo.* Nietzsche said that, and so did Pilate, Minneapolis Charles, and Herb from Lake-wood.

Paris, that postwar town of glories and drear, was a village with few automobiles, food shortages, black market. Faces that said war, occupation, suspicion, shame; the good bread and bad teeth were equal wonders to us. The mean temper of Parisians, hiding fun, put me at ease as the angry temper of New Yorkers, also often hiding fun, did not. I was an assiduous tourist. I walked the streets trod southward by Roman legions, and listened for their footsteps; I searched the rue St. -Jacques for the Pension Vauquer, where Vautrin challenged Rastignac to become a criminal cynic—I thought he might win me over, too; I learned French by reading Gide, Sartre, and Villon in the garden of the Russian Orthodox church at the corner of the Boulevard St. -Germain and the rue des Saints-Peres. My wife and I took bread, cheese, wine, and our solemn selves to lunch in the public gardens of this town of which we were the newest natives. We had always known it would be like this.

Stunned and goofy without pills, fasting, or champagne, we remained friends with Charles and Wendy, but lived on different schedules, marching to different drummers. They painted and practiced sex in a hotel near St. -Julien-le pauvre. We practiced marriage and philosophy at the Sorbonne and in our little hotel, rue de Verneuil, where I set out to study France, Europe, and world unity. By reading, walking, bicycling, and keeping my eyes open a lot, I would become an artist-philosopher, a stroller on two banks, unlike other men but brother to them all. I developed strong leg muscles, anyway.

And my pride! Saul Bellow winked at me! Lionel Abel explained the differences between Sartre and Heidegger while eating a croissant! James Baldwin, Jimmy forever, became my coffee-companion in addition to our neighbor in the next room at the Hotel de Verneuil! Otto Friedrich! H. J. Kaplan! Max Steele! Relatives and former relatives of Peggy Guggenheim! Eugene Jolas still alive! Alice B. Toklas pouring tea for shy young poets! Those who knew Joyce, those who still knew Gide and Hemingway. Some certified Frenchmen. Ponge. Henri Michaux. Merlau-Ponty. Citizens of Atlantis, subjects of Morphia, residents on the play-study program at the Café Bonaparte before they put in all the pinball machines; at the Café de Tournon, the Select, the ragged Dôme.

I made enemies, too, young writers, other writers, nothing-to-do Bohemians and hard-working gossipmongers, and some who were simply flabbergasted by my callowness (I'm on their side now). Harry Roskolenko called me a name-dropper. He was right. I had told him I was a good friend of Harry Hershkowitz, editor of *Death*, which was founded as the answer to *Life*, and he in turn was a good friend to Orson Welles . . .

An established surrealist, Philippe Soupault, then working for UNESCO, gave my wife the benefit of his insight into my character: *"Il est sadique."* To be called a sadist in French was impressive. How many of my friends in Lakewood or at Columbia had been called *sadique* by a man mentioned in every significant history of Paris literary Bohemia between the two wars? Maybe he knew something important, this poet, novelist, critic, teacher, manifesto-issuer who was vibrantly present at the founding of several movements.

"I hadn't thought of that," my wife said.

"Oui, oui, il est sadique," he said firmly, with the assurance of a man who has traveled with the surrealists, Aragon, Breton, Eluard, since the beginning, and now, wise and

weary after life's voyage, is resting his freckled, careworn hand on my wife's thigh.

Alas, I mongered a few opinions myself and merited some of my enemies. I stepped on the toes of a famous English publisher at the world premiere of *La Tour Eiffel Qui Tue,* a musical about a conspiracy by art students to eliminate this blot on the Paris skyline; no metaphor intended—he just had sensitive feet. Jean Genet took me to the Rose Rouge one afternoon to meet some friends (pickpockets, thieves, a singing quartet), and to keep the hands of a magician and true artist off my sensitive parts, I explained that I was not his *petit ami,* sir, I was just a plain old American student from le O-hee-o. Genet called me a *petit con* for embarrassing him before his comrades, and chased me down the street, shouting, *"Petit con! Petit con!"* while I occasionally turned and explained that I liked him very much, I loved his writing, I couldn't pretend to be his *petit ami;* and he listened to this literary criticism, appreciatively, gratefully, *comprehensively,* as the French almost say, and then screamed, *"Petit con!"*

It's easier to recall these excited encounters than the blessed hours when I ordered pieces of my mental debris into notebooks, and the debris seemed to obey orders, thus calling for more debris, more filters, more orders, more dizzy convictions. Isolated in the Paris mornings, coffee-crazy in the neighborhood cafés (it was always cold except in the cafés); and then on abruptly sunny afternoons, I ran down the rue de l'Université, teaching my wife to ride a bicycle. I had married a lady who spoke French, read good books, wasn't flat-chested, and played the piano—excellent IQ by actual repute—but whose mother had forbidden her to bicycle because she once scratched her legs in a thorny hedge. Well, now she had damn well better learn to hurt herself (*sadique* husband). I panted as I ran alongside, trying to steady the machine until she could do it herself, that delicate childhood task of balance, pump, play, and dodge the curbs and hedges with bold steering. You have will and motion; a hedge is a mere thorny natural object. Hope and skill do it, darling, no matter how your mother feared the blemish seeking out your knee.

The purest moments: those alone with the self and intention, when word and dream meet and the body staggers as it floats in the mind. I was I and only I; I had come into the world to tell each person who he was; I would set an example.

How easy to make fun of that person I was! But that other is still my secret self. When I meet a young man with the love light of vanity and desire in his eyes, I want to say *Brother,* though I know he is likely to see only a middle-aged competitor.

Those were sweet afternoons on the empty rue de l'Université, running slower, then as fast as I could, steadying a wobbly bicycle, past Seventh Arrondissement manses, gray stone, gray sky, blood hard in my throat, cobblestones, babies crying behind closed shutters. Suddenly I began having daymares about Lakewood, Ohio, and I was writing a novel about a man like the French resistance heroes I knew, nonetheless living in Lakewood. There was the nice joggling and loosening of memory occasioned by a sense of freedom among xenophobic Frenchmen who stared and saw not the despised Semite but the hated Coca-Cola–bringing American. It was not Lakewood, where everything was clear. But Lakewood was a complicated place and Parisian logic was a myth. I planted the spirit of *la Résistance,* of the perished heroes Jean Moulin and Yves Farge, in a mild home-bound bureaucrat on Hathaway Avenue, in Lakewood, Ohio.

From our hotel room we could look out onto the street and

see the little urn of painted clay placed against a wall at the corner with words *Ici est tombé pour La France . . . Roland LaPorte, âge 17.* A man had died in a pool of blood at that place only a few years ago. The *patron* at the hotel had seen it happen. Surely Roland LaPorte's family somewhere in these anonymous buildings were the ones who replenished the flowers in the urn. I watched for hours, and the fresh flowers appeared, but I never saw who put them there.

We were busy defining ourselves in this hotel—artists, students, Bohemians, *zazous*—not children and not adults, either. I was not the only one who sometimes wished he could be Roland LaPorte, age seventeen. That was the dramatic self-pity of the expatriate, sugar low in the blood, and it was unnecessary to imagine ourselves in his place to think of the family LaPorte, creatures of habit, buying flowers on Saturday and watching them dry to straw and fall scattered to the pavement after the week-end. I thought constantly about the war, which I had passed in schools and training, crawling under instructional bullets, while my cousins and friends died. Sometimes the memory of Roland LaPorte was a mere Francophile image, like the baguettes swung home in the evenings down the narrow corridor of the rue des Saints-Pères, the little bouquets of flowers carried with the bread, the intensely nervy, cursing drivers who tried to run down my bicycle with their 4-CV Renaults, the plaintive songs of Mouloudji, the tiny jokes and sentimentalities of Queneau and the tinny ones of Prévert, the bleary, aquiline sexuality of the girls at St.-Germain-des-Prés who were imitating Juliet Greco (one of them was Juliet Greco). We too could have breath that smelled of Gauloise Bleu and fast-moving Camembert, and take summer visitors to the Tabou or La Gargouille or the Rose Rouge, where the Frères Jacques sang songs by Sartre and gestured with their clown's white cotton gloves like an American minstrel act.

Provided the visitors paid. The money wasn't going as far as it was supposed to. I took to selling my clothes to North Africans who haunted the streets near Pigalle with their uprooted masks of woe and hope, looking for Americans whose money wasn't going very far. At first I thought I resembled these Arabs—brown, squinting, sharp elbows, knees, and teeth, spoiled mouth. Then I decided they were different from me. My only suit: well, it too was brown and unwelcome, anyway, and I never wore it. Sell it.

The man at the Clothing Café counted out a series of greenish francs. His tongue darted between his teeth, stinging each watermarked sheet as he snapped them out. He was mumbling numbers like a Moslem prayer. My wife looked at me as he counted. Maybe she was sentimental about my passing clothes. I wore GI leftovers most of the time, so what difference did it make?

I took the money. She took the money and cracked it in her fingers. She ran to the Algerian, who was leaving the café with my suit already strange to me, bundled under his arm. "Give me the money!" she cried.

"You have it, madame."

"Fausse! Fausse!"

He drew himself up with dignity. "It is as good as any money you can find in Pigalle."

"Give me that suit!" she said. No one moved. Men at the *zinc* with their morning cognacs and coffee stared into the mirror or at each other. Madame-in-black, the lady at the cage, was stacking coins. My wife rubbed her fingers across a bill and it smudged. "Give it back to me!" she screamed.

He tried to move out the door. "I'll get some other money."

"Leave the suit!"

"Take your hands off me! No woman touches me!" His rage was genuine. He was murderous. I was pulling her away, saying *Leave him, leave him alone, don't touch him;* and she wanted to claw his eyes out, to claw his flesh until she found non-counterfeit payment for what he owed her. I felt an insane pride in my passionate wife, and a crazy pity for the Algerian, wounded in his soul by this American girl who invaded his flesh, touched him, just because he was trying to steal my clothes. He was shrieking in Arabic now. We were strangers and enemies. His eyes were closed and red: how could they be both? He had a knife in his hand.

Delayed intense focus in the mind, like a film of disaster played again and again for clues to its meaning. We were pulling back slowly. He was dropping the clothes slowly. I took my wife's hand and dropped the fake money slowly. It fluttered across the floor. No one moved in the Pigalle café. He was backing out the door.

We were alone with my suit rumpled and dusty on the floor. The lady was crying. I took her home in a cab. "You're strong," I said.

"I am not, I'm not!" she cried.

"That was admiration. I didn't say you're tough. I meant it."

"I'm not, I'm not!"

"We could have gotten knifed. I'd just as soon let him have the suit."

"You think I'm stupid!"

"I didn't say that. But maybe you shouldn't stand on principle every time—"

"You don't like me!"

"Well, when you're right, you're strict, and maybe you shouldn't always be right—"

"Stupid, stupid, stupid world!"

We had a bitter quarrel in our tiny room at the Hotel de Verneuil; what begins as self-deprecation makes the worst of quarrels in marriage. After adrenalin strength and power in the Arab café in Pigalle, she wept out of girlish need of comfort. She wept for her father, dead when she was still a child. She wept for her mother—not the mother she needed. She wept for me.

I stroked her hair until her scalp must have felt sore, for she pulled away and gazed helplessly at me out of swollen eyes. "Now, now," I said.

In a dry and distant voice she said, "Maybe you're doing your best."

Could I say yes to that? Or no?

We were building our lives together. I couldn't admit I was only doing my best.

This time it was healed in the way young quarrels often are, and by morning I had convinced us both that I admired her marvelous resolution in a back street near Pigalle, daring to face a knife-wielding Arab. However, from now on I would sell my clothes by myself. There was a whiff of determination in her assault on the Arab which frightened me—a rage and pride which I put away with other recollections of dangerous rightness.

It reminded me of the righteousness of an older literary man—call him Francis Roan—who had just come back from attending a conference of the Committee for Cultural Freedom, where he urged the dropping of an atom bomb on Moscow. "They don't have it, we do," he said, meaning the bomb.

He had no doubts, he knew his intentions were pure. Therefore he could contemplate truths inaccessible to others. He could do the forbidden because it was he, a pure soul, who wanted to do it.

Someone at our table in the Royal St.-Germain argued with him. He replied in an irritable tenor, rasped with smoke, drink, too many meetings, too many disappointments. He was a great man of my boyhood; I had read his books in high school, and now here he was, dandruff flecking his shoulders, flesh heaving and sweating through a nylon shirt, telling us that the Communists had let him down and he wanted to finish them off for it. I changed the subject. Paris was something we could agree on. In love with Paris, a walking and bicycling city in those days, I asked about his own time in Montparnasse—the time of Hemingway, Fitzgerald, Robert McAlmon, James Joyce. "There were pretty girls then," he said jovially, and then more severely: "And geniuses. I don't see the pretty girls." He looked past the three young writers gathered for a word from an older master. "I don't see any geniuses. Nope, no geniuses, it's all gone dead."

Me! me! me! we wanted to cry.

"Oh, there really are some pretty girls," I said modestly.

"Nothing like it was. Nothing like it was, boy."

And in fact, for the one-time happy Marxist, whose monumental book had been called great by a generation, here in a new time nothing was as it had been, no girls beautiful any more; and as to the weedy young writers growing up about him, with their frayed faces turned toward him as toward the sun, he wanted only to make them wince. He was drinking sweet vermouth for his cough. He knew the remedy for each of his troubles, he had made his deal for remedies, and sweet vermouth for the cough was one which a corrupt world still provided him. Other remedies—a great book, a great love—were now out of reach.

He turned the conversation back to the atom bomb and his vision of its proper use; that is, as soon as possible. I was learning about people who want things their own way, now now now, just as they imagine it in some dream of revenge and final clarity. I envied their rightness and the charm of conviction it gives them. I marveled at the persistence of the will to do murder upon others in the interests of one's own cause, the only true and just one. I was also reading Montesquieu, great philosopher of the Enlightenment, who said of the African slaves bound for Haiti, "Their noses are so flat it is almost impossible to feel sorry for them," and managed to invest in the Compagnie des Indes, which monopolized the trade in black flesh. Francis Roan was saying, "It's them or us, western civilization or the monolith. Take Moscow and maybe they'll learn."

I'm not sure I like the young man who looked at the older writer and saw only a brutal fool. Perhaps he deserved no credit for the books I had admired. He wanted to murder a population, the race of his enemies. But I'm not sure I like the young man who gave him no shrift in his decline.

A few weeks later, celebrating the Fulbright award which had surprised me in Paris, I was staying with my friend Ben Johnson in Rome. He had given a story of mine to the Illustrissima ma Principessa Marguerite Caetani di Bassiano, born in St. Louis or Connecticut, U.S.A., who published a trilingual magazine called *Botteghe Oscure*. He telephoned to ask if she would like to meet me. "No," she said, "I don't like to meet writers unless I publish their work."

"Oh." He hung up. "She doesn't want to meet you unless she's publishing it."

"Oh."

A moment later the telephone rang again. "I'm publishing it," she said crisply. "Bring him around."

Half an hour later a valet with a silver tray and a check appeared at Ben's apartment, saluted, passed me the money, tucked the tray under his arm, and was gone. At teatime we climbed onto Ben's Lambretta and rode off to the castle of the literary princess, patron to Truman Capote, Dylan Thomas, Paul Valéry, and some now forgotten. Ben is a black man—not really black, of course—and so the urchins of Rome would scream "Tarzan! Tarzan!" at him as we scootered through the streets and plazas of hallowed Rome. It's true that he has good manners, like Lord Greystoke. The kids paid homage, and also thought he might cure hunchbacks by touching them.

Despite those days of depression and rationing after the war, the palace of the princess had the use of dry-cleaning, footmen, and food cards. We were bowed past doors by men in livery. Grand smoky portraits and sly clocks on tables with paws observed our progress. I waded through a snow-white carpet; it impeded the way. Ben took it more seriously. He leapt a snowbank of fur, and slid ingloriously, untarzanly, upon his rump. A footman extended one finger to help him up. When we found the princess in her cozy library, fire burning, she was in tennis shoes and my apprehension disappeared. She would be nice! She was just an American! "Thank you for liking my story," I said.

"I thought you were a Negro," she said. "Isn't Gold an, um, southern name?"

"No, I'm staying with Ben," I said, "but as you see by the color of my skin—"

"Yes. One lump or two? Lemon? Cream?"

I remembered Miss St.-Martin, my long-skirted patroness from West 11th Street. I was greedy enough to take all three, lemon, sugar, and cream. Good sense prevailed.

The lady was related, she said, to T.S. Eliot. She loved literature and writers. She had money, a magazine, a prince in the family—as husband—who seemed to own a lot of the land between Rome and Naples. Here we were all together on a pinnacle of literary elegance, despite her bobby socks and tennis shoes. We swore eternal correspondence. She was older than Miss St. -Martin and lacked the distraught daughter.

A few days later Ben led me to another literary gathering. "They're rounding up all the niggers in Rome to meet Richard Wright. You're invited."

We spent the day on Ben's Lambretta, stopping to spy through giant keyholes at monasteries or to drink Frascati. Ben translated the gossip around us as we toured the ancient city, his elegant head tilted, listening, laughing. He told me that Italian Jews often have the names of cities, such as Milano, or sometimes they translated Cohen into the Italian for Servant of God, Servadio. We visited ancient Jewish cemeteries. I remembered the few Sephardic Jews I had met in New York, and the tiny wedge of cemetery on West 11th Street, a still moment of stones and deaths and Spanish names.

At the reception for Richard Wright, the great man had a joyous grinning joke for everyone but me. To the white American, he was friendly. Later he told rambling anecdotes about his stardom in the movie of *Native Son* and teased and punched at people, making them easy, playing the buffoon.

It was a touching performance. Everyone had been frightened of him, so he made us laugh. There is a generous way to play the buffoon, and this generous sick man did it to help pass a moment which might otherwise have been painful. He gave us the right to feel superior to him, but no sensible man would accept the invitation. He had a complex nature, a complicated heritage, a good heart.

Italy without wife worsened the strain between Young Married and the difficult community of Bohemia. I was committed to conjugal strictness, the good kids from Cleveland and Detroit, and yet I was indecently unstrict and unformed, not such a good kid. I preferred loitering around, waiting for miracles, but I had to do the shopping. I had a notion of trust and understanding—only these things mattered between people—but I was mistrustful and impatient. A black painter said, "You're in the noose, man." An older philosopher said, philosophically, "Maybe you married kind of young." Jean Wahl, my advisor at the Sorbonne, said, *"Elle est mignonne, ta femme—et alors?"*

My wife said, "Sometimes I'm lonely, I don't know what I'm doing day after day."

"I missed you in Italy. I shouldn't ever go away without you," I declared, and believed the words I heard. O wanted to believe them! I held her tightly and rocked her to sleep. We wanted to be as strong as two sticks bound together, two aimless twigs wrapped in marriage and thus powerful, defended, a gathering.

One morning a delegation came to our room while I was supposed to be writing and my wife was out buying the cheese, bread, and tomatoes which we took to lunch with a bottle of wine in the Luxembourg or the Tuileries or the little garden of the Russian church at the corner of the rue des

Saints-Pères and the Boulevard St.-Germain. There was the Norwegian lesbian and the American film-maker and the novelist and the Belgian painter, a committee of my chosen colleagues, all knotted up with their solemn, high-level proposal. "Ve vill all cheep in," said the Norwegian girl, "a-okay? I arrange the ex-hee-beeshn."

There was a moment when I thought she meant paintings.

"You vill join us. You vill bring your vife." It sounded more like *fife*.

Such youthful solemnity—but it was all we had heard about Paris. Having read our Henry Miller, our Villon, Francis Carco, and Henri Murger, having seen the Opéra Comique version of *Les Mamelles de Tiresias,* and the folk singers at the Lapin à Gilles, it was now time for more basic Paris stuff. We were too young for tourist shenanigans at the Lido. We were too shy to lurk about the White Russian doormen on the rue Notre-Dame-de-Lorette. We were too free, independent, and unfettered to do anything that wasn't advanced, artistic, and shared with our gang.

"I'd like to go to an orgy," I said, "but I'm not sure my wife will let me."

"She too," said the stern lesbian.

"Not an orgy, a circus! Exhibition!" stated the pedantic novelist. "She won't have to do anything, necessarily," he added.

"I'd really like it," I assured him, my heart thumping.

Some of the fear came from the exhibition itself—me? that? a mere lad from Lakewood, Ohio?—but most of it had direct connection with my wife's response. I was bound by duty to consult with her. But it would be an affront even to mention the matter. But we believed in utter frankness with each other. Principle. Total honesty. But I had no right to insult her that way. But if I *didn't* tell her, that would be keeping secrets; and if I did, I would be betraying my base curiosity and worse—an invitation to violate her deepest convictions about purity and high purpose . . .

A bad night. She wept, I wept. Between times, I explained about the difference between an exhibition and an orgy, and then the tears flowed once more, a Cuyahoga, a Detroit river of tears, choked by the debris of intentions. At dawn we reached a statesmanlike compromise. I wouldn't mention it again. The subject would never be proposed in the better future which lay ahead. But I could continue to see these old friends, even if she personally didn't ever want to see them. She would forgive me this immoral loyalty—maybe. After all, she had forgiven Charles and Wendy, hadn't she?

Alone, I contemplated the quality of such forgiveness. I also had a public task to perform.

"I'd like to go to an orgy, excuse me, exhibition," I said to my friends like a little boy making his bedtime wish with folded hands, "but I don't think we will."

There were whispers which I heard as laughter down the halls of the Hotel de Verneuil. "Deuce, deuce again." I tried to sustain myself with pride against trilingual ridicule, but I felt like a fool. And then later: No, I have the right to do what I want to do, even if I don't want to do it. Er, I mean, after all, I'm a married man. I have the right to, um, a little disgrace in the eyes of my friends. This is not the group I need to belong to. They're not healthy and wholesome expatriate citizens like me and the missus.

She could now ride her new red bicycle straight and unwobbly down the rue de l'Université. How many of those perverts and fun-loving sex fiends could say they had successfully instructed a lovely young girl, once afraid to climb on, now willing to steer straight through the Seventh Arrondissement toward the Rodin museum on the rue de Varenne?

It wasn't as if I was, say, some driven Mr. Fergus, the neighborhood child-molester. But I was a child groom, in the noose, and as lonely as my wife, only making out from day to day. The dream of young marriage is to find meaning by gazing into each other's eyes. Eye to eye, soul to soul is all we need. It turns out that the world's noises cannot be drowned out, partly because the rumble also comes from the complex miniature civilization within each body—history, instinct, heart, brain, blood, the mysteries of eternal emission of signals between past and present, world and intention, hope and need and conscience. What folly to dream of wrapping these potencies in a gift of loving looks. Even loving actions, a loving plan can never be complete. Within cannot be done without, nor should it be, but lovers try and would-be lovers strive. Poor crazy kids, glaring tenderly into each other's eyes.

One gaze or another flinches under the effort. Romance is not a recipe for peace, nor romantic marriage a prescription for marriage. The crazy kids from Cleveland and Detroit sought to build their lonely fortress in the turbulent city, but the joys of Paris did not nourish that institution I had brought to Paris, marriage with the bright and nervous girl my parents would have liked if only they had liked her more. She was a lady with a good history of being a well-educated Jewish daughter. When her brief dream of romance ended, she might wisely have been prescribed for some old and distinguished literary man—the wife-of-writer, protecting, sheltering, jealously custodian of a reputation, the final wife, the perfect widow. On a grave she would have wept becomingly. She did not seem to be the wife for me, and wept becomingly because it was too soon for me to jump into the grave.

Our quarreling echoed my quarrels with my parents, who also asked that I be something else. Together these quarrels continued the dissolution of my last chance to be the nice son from Cleveland. I celebrated my wife's success in learning to balance a bicycle. I did my Dance of the Crazed Bicycle Instructor, lumbering against a streetlamp. This was Paris, wasn't it? This was freedom, wasn't it? We were the crazy kids, and we were surely the first couple ever to ride bicycles and then make love whenever we felt like it.

Beneath my mask of buffoonish ease, studied like an inspired instruction from Richard Wright, there lay another creature which felt sullen and brooded. Surely Mr. Wright sometimes felt sullen and brooding, too. There are always afterthoughts when things go only as well as possible.

Shyly one morning my wife interrupted this modified stoical state. She had a bottle with a Specimen in it. The doctor said . . . and if the rabbit and the specimen interacted with proper enthusiasm . . .

We embraced. She was finally forgiven for not wanting to attend the exhibition with me. Unlike those friends, who were merely artists and free spirits, we might soon be parents. I knew my duty. "Where's my bicycle?" I pedaled furiously away, bearing the warm paternal burden, across the Seine to a medical laboratory on the rue de Rivoli. On the Pont Neuf a pantleg caught in the bicycle chain and I was thrown to the pavement, but arose merely bruised, protecting the precious bottle by lifting it in my right hand like the torch of liberty. Secretly I was convinced that the bottle already contained an invisible infant.

A day later I picked up the report from the lab. *"On a sacrifié le lapin,"* it began elegantly, one has sacrificed the rabbit, and continued with the good news. Yes. Yes, we were prospective parents. "Would you like to take the rabbit home?" a lovely assistant asked me. She was petite, white-gowned, and in my joy I wanted to do French things with her. "Many people offer themselves a festive dinner, best with a light Chablis."

But I returned without the ritual rodent. My own ears were pink. My wife and I celebrated by taking sausages, choucroute garni and La Slavia beer, *chez* Lipp at St. -Germain-des-Prés. "You'll have to give up smoking, lots of red meat, vegetables, oranges," I informed her.

"Mm," she said dreamily, not quite listening.

We were happy. She had a right to say no to Bohemians, circuses, orgies. We had invented a better way of life. We were the first in the Hotel de Verneuil to think of having children. We had stumbled onto our discovery—perhaps on one of our good bicycling afternoons, perhaps during one of our many reconciliations. Smugly I reported my fantasy: I wanted her to cook the rabbit with a fine Chablis. She shivered at my masculine lust for very horrible suggestions. I worried only an instant, basking in conjugal love, over the fact that the idea came from a little French lab technician with bruised eyes and a sharp-toothed smile. My skinned knee stung against GI woolens. As a father and responsible, I would have to keep my bicycle in good repair.

When we returned down the rue Jacob and the rue de Beaunes to the Hotel de Verneuil, the door to our room was ajar. Someone had entered and taken the carton of Pall Malls. Later I saw Toke, the American film-maker, smoking a king-sized cigaret in the hall near the WC. He knew he would eventually find me there.

"Are those Edith's cigarets?" I asked.

He laughed.

"What kind of idiocy is that?"

He laughed.

"You stupid-ass creep," I said. "By the way, we're having a baby."

He came toward me with an intense and solemn face. He removed the cigaret from his mouth. "Oh Jesus, Herb, that's great. Oh Christ, that's wonderful." He touched me on the shoulder. A light was dawning, an inner radiance. "So that's why you didn't go to the exhibition. Shit, it was a bore anyway. I didn't have a girl, but it was a terrific bore, but that's why . . . Oh Christ, I'm sorry." He stopped for a moment by that gurgling closet and threw his arms around me. He pressed the *minuterie* to get some extra radiance on the subject. One watt of light. "Ah, that's swell, he said. "Blessings! Lemme tell people, okay?"

The next morning the remainder of the carton of Pall Malls lay wrapped in a copy of *Le Monde*, along with a bottle of wine, at the crack of our door. The label on the wine said Châteauneuf du Pape, 1949, instead of what we were used to, Guaranti 12%.

I carried the cigarets back to the sleeping Toke's door and left them there. She shouldn't smoke anyway. I kept the wine.

I told her what I had done and she ran to rescue her cigarets.

"Don't run, don't run!" I hissed as she hurried barefoot down the hall.

"They're mine," she said when she returned.

But I didn't want this to be our first quarrel since we knew she was carrying our child. Not the Arab for whom I had felt sorry when he recoiled at her hands on his almost-real money, not my fellow would-bees, disapproving of the bourgeois couple in the room next door, but this fretful lady was to be the mother of that flesh and spirit we shared. Who was this child and to what community did it belong? It was ours and we its, his, hers.

• • •

In his office near the Etoile our obstetrician kept an illuminated statue of Maternity rising from a floor mirror, like Poseidon from the sea. While waiting for Motherhood to come ashore off the mirror, we happened to make some friends outside the close world of international free spirits. I had a French cousin, survivor of the war and occupation. We met a man who could barely talk because of damage done his pituitary glands in a concentration-camp experiment; his jaw, his tongue, ears, hands, and feet were growing inexorably, until his tongue would choke him to death. Acromegaly was its musical name. When I shook his hand, my hand lay in a great horny wrapping; there was nothing to grip. The distorted face looked apologetic; it regretted. I've forgotten his name; I remember acromegaly. He in turn introduced me to an old man, Schwartz, who was writing a book about the Jewish artists killed by the Nazis, including photographs of them and their work and short histories of their truncated careers. He was also a survivor, but gave up his own painting to perform this act of penitence and homage. "I lived. I lived," he said, still not believing it. "I'm alive."

I wished that I could speak Yiddish. I couldn't. I spoke Russian and French with the refugees from everywhere, incomprehensibly cast up alive in Paris, some with heavy new flesh loose on their skeletons, some puzzled ones taking up the strands as if nothing had happened. A few even thought of saving their money and having the tattoo removed (Gestapo men were tattooed in a different place). The ones I knew best lived permanently in the sight of their history. Not all of them walked with crippled pituitary glands, hunched like terrified wrestlers, apes in blinding glasses, but all had ears cocked and eyes distanced by unbearable recollections. They seemed to be listening for the past to be rescinded. The man with swelling nose, ears, hands, feet, tongue, came to sit with his arms dangling between his legs. He talked to me about a Polish city which no longer existed. I strained to understand the guttural detonations of French, Yiddish, and cracked Russian. He leaned forward on the edge of the bed, his hands now resting like half-stuffed sacks on his knees, telling me that Jews do not believe in a hell after death, not even for their enemies. The man with acromegaly said that occasionally the rest of the world offers Jews a hell on earth which even Jews cannot avoid. Hitler did it best. Hitler succeeded. But through the extraordinary victory of Hitler, the survivors were confirmed in their knowledge that hell on earth is the only one they have to deal with; there can be nothing worse; heaven, if any, will be found on earth, too.

When he explained about hell, an ironic crevice parted the slabs of lips, what was left of the power to smile. When he explained about the Polish town which no longer existed, there was a glimpse of the vision of heaven; a glitter in eyes buried in the ridges and valleys of turbulent bone: *"Le pain est bon, monsieur. Le Shabbat—krasivi."*

A bluish cartilaginous tongue. A voice croaking and breaking to make the unfinished American know what he knew. Hitler's punishment is that he reinforced the stubborn characters of Jews.

And yet my wife was swollen and heavy, and she was happy, as was I, as we were with each other at that moment. Peace to the couple, peace to ourselves. I sat with the old man Schwartz and his album of murdered artists, puzzling over the photographs and reproductions, trying to remember all these men and women. Dead. Dead. Dead. The book was written in Yiddish. I asked Schwartz to translate his summaries for me. They were spare, mild, and said not so much as the eyes looking out of the book into mine. Those eyes were relics; they existed no place any more. They existed for Schwartz. I asked him to read the dedication of his book: *To the gypsies.*

"Why?" I asked.

"When I was in Auschwitz," he said, "I met a gypsy. He said: We will all die. You Jews will die. We will die. But the world will remember the Jews." This ferocious old man Schwartz, collecting his Yiddish album to be published by subscription from Jews in America, said, "I want them to remember the gypsies. I want the gypsies to be remembered because no one will remember them, either."

As our child was born at the Hôpital Foch in a slate-gray workingman's quarter of Paris, I stood outside the door and heard a nurse screaming at my wife, *"Poussez! Poussez, madame!"* Those moans and shrieks were strangers to which I had given birth along with the child. I marveled at them, and wondered why so much pain and pushing, starting so young, just to get into the world, and it doesn't stop there.

"Petite fille! Je vous félicite, monsieur."

We held our daughter and looked at something outside ourselves. What we felt we called happiness, but that's only a name. To know about the child and weakness is to begin to know about men and power—Charles and Wendy, Saul Bellow and the Arab counterfeiter who hated to be touched by the fingers of women, Philippe Soupault and the Red-crazed novelist, Ben Johnson and Richard Wright, Schwartz and the man who explained about hell, power and powerlessness and the human state in between, and the ones whom I now came to treasure equally with my own life, of which I was becoming the custodian. Roland LaPorte, the murdered Jews and gypsies, and my daughter Ann.

My first novel was taken by a publisher in New York. We

went back to Cleveland to live. In my mad pride—new father, new novelist—I expected to find a statue to my glory in the Public Square, between Higbee's Department Store and East Ohio Gas, next to the hectic Civil War heroes on their horses. They hadn't finished the casting. While waiting, I found a job managing a hotel on Prospect Avenue. It was the time of Korea, Senator Joe McCarthy, the Eisenhower mumble. I wanted my child to grow up an American. I hoped to discover both what that was and what it could be.

9

My novel appeared. I received a telegram from a generous editor. My picture was not on the three-cent stamp, nor was my pigeon-encrusted statue to be found in the Public Square. Writing the book in Paris had been magic, but the novel itself was unmagical; it creaked and groaned with flexings and intentions. I was a graduate student trying to crash like an icebreaker in March through the glacial freeze of Lake Erie. I mean *serious*. I mean choked with metaphor and symbol. I mean polluted.

Blessed amnesia put the book itself out of my mind, but I still felt my body caught in the rhythm of mornings with a notebook in a damp room or a steamy café, that sculptural exhilaration of the physical act, writing. A bad book, I learned, can be written with the same sweet joy as good ones. I had to learn what everybody knows.

Despite my nostalgia for Paris, where on our last day my wife and I had walked back and forth across the Pont des Arts, unwilling to quit the bridge over the Seine mildly fluttering below, back and forth in the deepening evening, and she said, "We'll never come back again, we'll never come back together," and wept for the end of something, to be home in Cleveland was a liberation. I returned to the scenes of childhood nightmare and found myself a mere married man with one child, then with two children, with a job, with another novel in another notebook (a better one, pray God), a new life in the jazz clubs of Cleveland, Short Vincent Street, smoky Moe's Main Street, peculiar new part-time jobs, editing an entertainment magazine, teaching, night-clerking in a hotel, not sleeping very much. After the programmatic freedom of Paris, stubborn and familiar Cleveland was a new city to me. I felt tall enough to see from Lakewood, where there were no Jews, to the east side, where my relatives lived. I began to suspect the cost of my childhood quarantine.

There were also some nesting artists and writers, that international Bohemia dispersed like the Jews nearly everywhere, and the little roads and paths near Wade Park, near University Circle, around the Murray Hill Italian ghetto and down East Boulevard, were as romantic and poignant as the rue Chevalier-de-la-Barre or the Place de Furstemberg. I haunted interfaith pizzerias or Cedar Avenue soul-food diners, just as I had smacked my Fulbright lips over onion soup at dawn in Les Halles or *foie haché,* chopped liver, in the ancient ghetto of the rue Vieille du Temple, rue des Rosiers. History didn't have to be old to be historical. Yesterday, when the Hungarians came to the south side and Magyar Village, when my father rode his White Motors truck to Lakewood, was as elusive and sheltering of its meaning as the time, a mere span earlier, when the Roman legions marched with their short swords into Lutèce, Lutetia, where the Parisii dwelled in a village smaller than Sandusky-on-the-Lake. Paris reminded me of my childhood in Lakewood, and now Lakewood gave resonance to my other childhood as a newly married man and skinny father pedaling his bicycle in Paris.

The Cleveland School of painters was renowned beyond Lorain and Sandusky on the west, Erie and Harrisburg in Pennsylvania, particularly for watercolors. An old German bookseller, Richard Laukhoff, once a friend to Hart Crane and Ernest Bloch, stepped out of his shop in the Colonial Arcade to show me the Blue Boar Cafeteria. "Iff zey eat zair, zey can buy books. But no! Zey eat over zair"—pointing to a paneled businessmen's rathskeller where zey were ordering book-depriving steaks and steins of cold beer instead of bargain trays of steamed tuna fish at the Blue Boar. Now I knew why *Birth of a Hero* disappointed my publisher and me. Tuna fish and creamed chicken were too great a sacrifice for the lovers of literature among Thompson Products executives.

Young poets and novelists chuffed and gasped like beached whales in Cleveland, but kept busy starting magazines, teaching, quarreling, finding jobs for their wives, and showing art movies in the parlor of a natural organizer who lived in a federal housing project under the High Level Bridge. We shared the costs of film rentals. We drank wine and played guitars and there were girls who hung around. We who were married held hands with our wives for protection against temptation. It was togetherness time, that curious moment of the early fifties—the cold war, the creeping baldness of tract houses, North Korean stubbornness, manias about subversion and the President forever smiling. I harried a notebook with plans for a wild manifesto, "The Protocols of the Elders of Bohemia," but even this international non-conspiracy, this local branch sticking out of my back pocket, would never provide the sense of community and purpose I required. Writing novels would not do enough. Nor would wife and children. Both did something, but there must be more.

The poems and secret journals did something, but there must be more.

Shaving, I looked in the mirror mornings, and took the measure of alternating dreams of evasion and responsibility, and with dread and longing gazed into the eyes of my daughters, and watched my father burrow furiously into his old age, and quarreled and had secrets from my wife, and there were discoveries of friendship, and there must be more, too.

We had a yard for the babies. My parents visited us twice a week. I wrote advertisements for committees opposed to the execution of the Rosenbergs, orated at meetings against the outrages of Senator McCarthy, had a part-time job teaching, had a full-time job as a night clerk, wrote my book while the drunks and whores seethed in the hotel about me, was visited by the FBI, and now it was time to leave Cleveland again. I sat in a library with a list of fellowships and found something to fit what I thought I could do. The meeting of France and Africa—why not?

It wasn't the FBI that put me in that library, crafting my message to the committee of judges of philosophy, literature, French, and how smart I might yet prove to be. It was my beloved native turf of Cleveland. After two years of it, oh, time to clear out.

The Republic of Haiti was a land without Jews except in myth and memory. There was no congregation and no cemetery, but there were a few visitors. There were some visiting

American Jews, two Israelis. There was no community, no rabbi, no shared spirit—this lack was nothing strange to me. I had lived my life with no Jewish community, no Jewish leadership except habits dimly revealed in my family, no religious portion. A few habits, and their shadows in my father and mother, must have given me the connection with the past we all need to survive. My father was a man mysterious to me, though reconciliation is a kind of understanding and we reconciled in Cleveland. An avenue of blood was my link with history, and as I came back to him in time, I also went forward with my children into the history of the future.

The barrenness of history without connection became as demanding as hunger or thirst. Neither the orgiasts of Paris nor the foreign-movie subscribers of Cleveland had given me this community. My friends, the future beatniks of Morningside Heights, were turning inward, round and round, on an axis which neither wine nor marijuana, sex or abstinence, ecstatic poetry or stoic philosophy could make other than what it was—lovely, lonely, lost, and lorn Bohemia. Schwartz and the man with acromegaly had come to be closer to me in Paris than my brothers-in-Fulbright. In Haiti I continued a persistent, half-conscious search for the Jew in myself, and it began as something little more than a fantastic paradox— to find Jews in the land without Jews. Even in this desolate Caribbean island, suffering from the deepest poverty and isolation, its Christianity smudged over by voodoo, there remained an imagination of Jews; for me and, as I learned, for others.

In the rank, oily harbor of Port-au-Prince, glistening black boys dived for coins, snatching at the glint of silver, seeming to turn like playful dolphins for the pleasure of the tour ships. The smoke of charcoal fires lay over the white heap of a city built on hills like Naples, Haifa, and San Francisco. The lizards played up walls and across ceilings, darting after flies. Beyond the port, the town was sleepily insomniac, drinking coffee and rum-coca to stay awake, but to see it as a tourist was to see frantic commerce, subtle sexual gaming, a struggle to stay alive and feel vivid in the heat.

What was I doing in Haiti? The traditional or curriculum-vitae answer is: studying the intersection of France and Africa, lecturing about literature under U.S. study grant. Another answer would be: bored with marriage, desiring to break the habit of suburbia, wishing to ease wife's spirit by providing distraction and cheap servants. The deepest answer is that the dreams of childhood are always with us. *I can fly. I can find perfect love. I can do what I choose to do, be what I choose to be.* In the hunt for buried treasure (in which I nearly died of malarial jaundice), in adventures among white magic, black magic, and harsh strangers, I could discover the possibilities of that harsh stranger which was my self. And following along, grinning at me with big teeth, was the devil of a question from my earliest childhood: What is a Jew and why am I this thing?

Stand far from it, stand close. I sought an adequate response, along with love, riches, and mastery over the straw wiggling in my fingers. Pursuit of those matters would do until the truth came along.

I shipped out as a scholar assigned to the Université d' Haiti. The School of Music in those days of 1954 consisted of one professor, a Cuban guitarist whose sister was the mistress of the Président de la Republique. The university was a complex of termite-ridden wooden buildings, barracks, and gingerbread houses, but Haiti had an adequate medical school and the crowded school of law required by French tradition. There was a steady stream of anthropologists come to study voodoo, village culture, and the marketing system. In the countryside, another synonym for white man was "anthropologue," just as a Haitian educated abroad was known in Creole as "oun masters-of," indicating that he was no doubt a Master of Something-or-other from Columbia University. I happened to be a white master-of.

Haiti divided the peoples of the world into three races—black, mulatto, and white. An occasional oriental visitor was just another rich white man. The real and practical social discord, between black and mulatto, was played against an abstract historical world warfare between Haiti and everyone else. A few Haitians believed, as did one of my friends among the coffee-drinkers of the Cénacle des Philosophes in the village of Kenscoff: "Haiti is the third force. After the United States and Russia destroy civilization, Haiti will make peace between them."

"Ah!" said Monsieur Bonfils, rural judge and coffee merchant, the brown instructional index finger uplifted. *"Peut-être avec l'aide de la Chine Jaune! Ce sont, n'est-ce pas, presque des gens de couleur."*

I rediscovered an odd condition in Haiti. I was first of all a white man without qualification. In Paris American, in Port-au-Prince white. Coddled or resented, teased or accepted, I was a member of the group called *"blancs,"* a name which included all foreigners. Nothing is pure on this earth, of course, and even black Americans—foreign is dominant—were often called *"blancs."* And a rich black Haitian could be transformed by Haitian optical nerves into a mulatto or a *"griffon"* or one of the hundred-odd other classifications for someone with mixed blood and complicated skin, nose, hair, lips. And money, the magic color filter.

The dentist, market women, and Haitian bureaucrats were missing something in their definition of me as white like all other whites. But there was no Jewish community, no Jewish life. Even that most primary and final sign of Jewish history, as of all histories, was lacking—no Jewish cemetery, no Jewish place in a cemetery. A Jew might run and hide, history is full of that, but the cemetery remains, or the place where the cemetery once stood, or the memory of that place. None. No graveyard, no place, no memory of the place which never was. And yet, as it happened, even here, in this lovely, forsaken corner of the world, Jews had come out of hope, desperation, and in one case at least, perhaps simple curiosity.

Before I found the traces of Jewry, I found the anti-Semites, refugees from their crimes, a Gestapo informer from Paris who became my good friend and companion ("Get me into the States, can't you? Surely *you* can!"), and a Pétainist colonel in exile. Odd to meet the evidence of my own history first in the form of its enemy, the exiles biting their nails, biding their time in a backwater of time. And then I found Haitians like my friend Jean Berlin, a handsome engineer and traveler, tall as a Watusi, with a cackling hysterical laugh when he described the origin of his distinguished Roman Catholic family: "Berlin! A Jew from Berlin came here to trade in coffee! He left a family of brown coffee merchants in Jacmel, in Jeremie, and another wife here in Port-au-Prince, and now Bair-lin is a fine old Gallic name for a family *croyant et bien-pensant,* all of us married in the cathedral. I'm the only one who tells the truth, my friend."

He knew nothing of being Jewish except that his rebellion against the conservative old family consisted in saying, Yes, I am. *I am!*

Through my friend Berlin, I met an accountant, a morose black man with a degree from a school of business in Philadelphia and a mania for recounting the days of his persecution. Restaurants, doormen, professors, women had all treated him like a *Negro*—"*Moi qui est Haitien!*" he cried.

Except in the purgatory of Philadelphia, he despised Haiti, the peasantry, and the Jews; and his name was Cohen.

When he confided one evening that the Jews are at the root of all the trouble in Haiti and the world, I said to him, "I am a Jew." He looked at me blankly through his red-rimmed eyes, as if he had never seen one before. "And you, with your name," I said.

"My grandfather came from Jamaica!" he shouted.

"You must have had a Jewish grandfather in there someplace," I said.

"You're making that up! . . . How did you know?"

"Cohen."

"*Cohen?*" he asked. To him Cohen was the name of a Catholic Haitian accountant. I explained that the Cohanim were priests and he was descended from priests and princes.

"Priests don't have children," he said irritably.

"Do you really think Jews caused all the trouble in Haiti?"

"No, not all," he said, "but the wars, the world wars, all the wars hurt us, too."

There was a black double ledger between his secret Jewish grandfather and his desire to provide an explanation for trouble and sin in the world. I could nag at him with facts, scandalize him with my own history, but I could never change his accounting and put Cohen, the Haitian accountant, in touch with Cohen, the man with an ancestor who did not begin the line in Jamaica. He had horn-rimmed glasses, owlish eyes with reddened conjunctiva, pockmarked black skin, and a Jew-hating heart which was only stopped a moment from its need by the information, which he knew already, that his name meant something grave in his past. He was not descended from an infinite line of Jamaican mulattoes. Someplace back there in the accountant's genes wandered a Jew.

"Priests don't have children," he mumbled, "but of course

princes do. That's just a theory you have, however. I studied the Jews very carefully in Jamaica and Philadelphia."

"If you knew more about the troubles of the world," I told him, "you'd be safer from them."

"J'en ai eu, des difficultés."

"Try to learn what they come from."

Not safe, but safer. I didn't add the maybe which would only confuse a black Roman Catholic Cohen in search of clear definitions.

There were others like him, of course, good Mass-going Haitians with names like Goldenberg or Weiner, or with Sephardic names like Silvera. The legend of Jewish ancestry might make some of them giggle, but it was even more fantastic and unreal than the feudal French names of other Haitians. The Duc de Marmalade was one of the courtiers of the mad emperor Faustin Soulouque, and the hamlet of Marmalade, reachable by burro, still exists in the scrub jungle center of Haiti. Faustin the First (there was no second or other) named four princes, fifty-nine dukes, ninety counts, two hundred barons, three hundred and forty-six chevaliers. Later the deputies and senators also became barons. Massacre and forgetfulness have ended most of these lines.

In Jacmel, a tiny town on the sea with an unpaved Grand Rue, perhaps once a week a police jeep scattered the traffic jams of black Haitian pigs, flailing dust; the pigs are as skinny and speedy as dogs. There was also a *pension*, telephones and electricity which rarely worked, the mud-and-straw huts of a spoiled African village—and in this place, Jacmel, I found a Jewish tailor. A few elegantly carpentered Haitian dream houses floated above reality like candy visions, slats and shutters, parapets and magic cages filled with lizards or birds, but Monsieur Schneider lived in a dwelling only a few boards and nails separated from a *caille-paille,* the country hut of mud and straw. He did his work at a hand-treadled machine in the dusty street, his head tilted to one side to favor his good eye, his joints swollen and his body twisted by arthritis. He was old and wore rags, like many Haitians, but the rags were sewn into the blurred shape of a European shirt and suit. It was too hot for such formal etiquette. He was one of three white people in the town. In the air around him, like the insects and the animals—the little black Haitian pigs that ran and even barked like dogs—eddied the members of his extended family, the mixed African and Semitic, some dark and some light, children and adults, wives and grandchildren.

With no authority but our common color and knowing his name, I spoke with him, first in English. No English, but he understood that I was asking him if he was a Jew. Was *I*? Yes. *Oui.* A flood of Yiddish poured out of his head. I spoke no Yiddish. He looked at me as if to doubt my sanity. A Jew I said, and spoke no Yiddish? He tried Creole. We settled on French, which he spoke in a Yiddish accent, with Creole words and phrases. He believed I was what I said I was, for otherwise what gain for either of us? Who needed to tell lies here, so far from the Czar's police? He was a shriveled old man, kicking amiably at the grandchildren—children?— playing about the treadles of his Singer machine. The treadle was cast with scrolls and Art Nouveau symbols in iron polished by his bare feet. To do honor to our conversation, he slipped his feet into sandals soled with sliced and shaped rubber tires and sisal uppers.

He did not have the look of a man who asked deep questions but he stared at me from his one good eye. "What's a Jew—?" he asked.

I had no answer until he finished the question.

"—doing in Jacmel?"

His face, shriveled against sunlight, shriveled by age, blotched and deeply freckled, looked like a dog's muzzle. "Why is a Jew *living* here?" I asked him in return.

"My home," he said. "Living? You call this a life? My wife is dead. I have another wife. My children and grandchildren."

"Would you forgive the question? How did you happen to settle in Jacmel?"

He pumped furiously at the machine. He was fixing a seam, a simple matter, but he gave it all his concentration. Then he looked up and squinted around at me. I had moved so he wouldn't be staring into the sun and he winked at so much consideration, Jew to Jew.

"Jacmel," he said. "And where else is there?"

Jeremie, St.-Marc, Cap Haitien, Port-au-Prince, Port-de-Paix—that's all.

"Were you Polish?" I asked him.

"Russian."

"So were my parents. Why didn't you go to the United States?"

"Ah," he said. "Because I wanted to learn the French and Creole languages, *c'est vrai?*"

"*Non,*" I said.

"Because"—and he spread wide his arms—"I had adventure in my heart?"

"No."

He put down his cloth, he stood up, he was a tiny old man with one dead eye. He put his face close to mine, pulled at the lid of the dead eye as if he were stretching a piece of cloth, and said, "I went to Ellis Isle, maybe your father did too. But he didn't have a sick eye. At that time it was infected from the trip. They sent me away. And then I wandered, no place to go, so instead of killing myself I came to Haiti."

Stupid to be oppressed by a sick eye from a generation before I was born. "I'm sorry," I said.

He started to laugh. It was not the dry, fearful, old-man's Jewish laughter of my uncles in Cleveland. It was a rich, abandoned, Haitian old-man's laughter. He clutched at his pants for luck. "You see these children? You see all the brown Schneider children in Jacmel? Many died, my wives often die, but look what I have done. I have proved God is not malevolent. He let me live, He let some of these children live. God is indifferent, but I have shown, not proved, but *demonstrated* that He is not malevolent."

"If you believe, God is not evil, merely all-powerful."

He put his face down, he reached in his pocket for a cube of sugar and held it up to my face. "If He were all-powerful, then He would be evil. He could not allow what He allows. Coffee? You like good Haitian coffee? Marie!" he shouted into the *caille-paille. "Café pou l'blanc!"*

I drank coffee with the tailor and his new wife, who said not a word as she sat with us. He sucked cubes of sugar and drank his coffee through them.

"I have a few books," he said, "but I was never a scholar. My uncle was a rabbi, I think my brother was going to be a rabbi, but"—he shrugged—"I never found out what he became. You're not a rabbi?"

"No."

"It's not so ridiculous. I heard once there are rabbis who don't speak Yiddish."

"I don't speak Hebrew, either."

"Then you couldn't be a rabbi, could you? But you speak other languages."

I wanted to give him answers and ask questions, but we drank coffee and made tiny conversation. We were two Jews speaking a mad polyglot in the town of Jacmel, which few

123

ever visit, even if they live in the nearby villages of Carrefour Fauché, Bassin Blue, or Bainet. Jacmel is the end of the world, with a dusty street and a crowd of people. He didn't offer to show me about the village. We sat in his portion of the street in front of his door. His arthritis confined him to his sewing machine and his house of wood, mud, and straw. His house had a floor of hewn slats; it was not just a *caille-paille*. His wife watched us with mournful eyes, as if I might take him away from her, but time was taking him away faster than I could. We had little to say across the many years and many lives between us except to give each other greetings in the town of Jacmel.

When I said goodbye, dizzy with coffee, he stood up painfully, and I saw a small thin bent brown man, a creature neither Russian nor Jewish nor Haitian, something molded in time's hands like a clay doll. He put out his hand and said in a cracked voice, laughing at the peculiar word he must have pronounced for the first time in years: *"Shalom!"*

I would return to Jacmel to try to learn what living in this place meant for a Russian Jew, but although I did come back to visit, I was still only a tourist. A few years later there was a hurricane which devastated the village, and now, with another half a generation gone by, I wonder what of Schneider's mark on life can still be felt there. Has one of the mixed-blood Schneiders learned to sew and use the treadle? Have they scattered? How many survive? No matter; he had many sons and daughters; something of Jewry has surely been sown in this corner of Haiti which is forsaken, like the rest of the world, by an indifferently fructifying God.

It seems that I had gone hunting for Jews, but in fact I was unaware of my desire. I was busy with wife and children. We kept a lizard in a cage, warning burglars of what our magic could do to them. I was writing, reading, floating, studying, learning about Haiti, not about Jews. I was drifting and lazing with an island's self-sufficient timelessness.

But when a Jew happened, I was alert. It was an odd nostalgia which chilled and wakened me; I didn't know why. I know why: it returned me to myself.

I met the old Russian Jew Lazaroff living with his Haitian wife and his library on the mountain leading from Port-au-Prince above Kenscoff to the Fôret des Pins. He was unused to speaking with visitors, and it was a skill he didn't need any more. He gave me coffee; he smiled without speaking when I looked at his books and said, "I've read that . . . I've read that one . . ."

"Please, if you would like to borrow?" he said at last.

"No, thank you, I have enough books. You've been here long?"

"Long," he said.

"You plan to stay very long?"

"Forever," he said.

"Why?"

He shrugged. "That's not very far away."

I met the French Calmann who had suffered under Hitler and chose not to suffer under the Soviet occupation of France. "If that happens," I said, "Haiti won't be safe, either."

"Haiti will be safer," he said stubbornly. "This time I've done all I can."

These flight-obsessed men, cutting their losses, limited their gains to nothing but survival. They served their time on earth as a dizzy bewilderment. Then it happened that I came to know Shimon Tal, the fisherman, who had more than survival in mind.

There was a small colony of foreigners attracted to expatriation in this dreamy corner of the world by island ease, drink, isolation, or porous laws. They could live with eleven-year-old girls or drink Rum Barbancourt, smoky and rich as brandy, or buy the police for whatever odd quirks or against whatever odd crimes they had committed elsewhere. It was a good place to hide the self, and perhaps, in voodoo, excess, and wildness, even in odd new disciplines, also a place for finding selves. There were plenty of local fishers of souls, and plenty of souls to be fished—often, of course, the fishers and the fish were identical. Doc Reser, a retired Marine sergeant, was now a voodoo priest; a wild white pelt on his chest, much drink, little wily red barroom eyes; and old Dan Cassidy, once a fashion photographer in Paris and New York, who collected all his wives from one family, marrying the girl, divorcing her when she turned fifteen, looking toward her younger sister, trying again, one more good shot for true love; many others. There were the international bureaucrats, United Nations study groups, American military missions, Jesus missionaries, Belgian and Breton priests, chic Episcopalians, CARE officials trying to keep the milk away from the weevils and the politicians, researchers on detached service from the Katherine Dunham dance troupe, entranced addicts dug into a good connection, sly advisors and profiteers, apprentice white gods, retired white gods, a Swedish geologist looking for gold, oil, tungsten, or hemp—anything salable—aging Greenwich Village ladies who loved black men, or at least hoped to be loved in return, a few winsome homosexuals, political exiles with a purchase on the police, escapees from Devil's Island, a friendly Gestapo informer, wreathed in engaging boyish smiles, and, of course, the wandering students, and anthropologists who wore castoff World War II clothes and were forever looking for an authentic voodoo ceremony, finding a staged one. And settling for an authentic cockfight.

A lovely high-living international lady named Shelagh reminded me, with only the slightest touch of malice, just enough to keep awake in the hot season, that I might like to meet a fellow Jew. He was a United Nations fishing expert, an Israeli, and she described him as weathered and quiet as a farmer. "I like him, he's funny. He pretends he's asleep all the time because he's, you know—shy?"

I'd heard of that.

She had met him at an obligatory meeting for a UN official; he was hiding from the foreign colony. The notion of a shy Israeli, of Middle European ancestry, teaching this island people to fish, made me smile, too. Maybe he wasn't shy, only embarrassed.

I didn't find him at any United Nations or American Aid drinkfests, but eventually we met. I was visiting the Damiens agriculture station outside Port-au-Prince. His Haitian "counterpart" (trainee), Monsieur Gerard, a gleaming, very polite graduate of the Damiens School, hung at his elbow as if his every motion gave hints about the puzzling folkways of fish. The counterpart might learn how fish bit and bred, swarmed in schools and took to the rushes, by studying this white man's gestures. We toured the ponds—carp, tilapia, fry, mature fish—and Tal explained about protein starvation and the bounty which could be provided by the sea and also by rivers, marshes, ditches, and ponds.

Then he asked to come to visit us. When he did, without Monsieur Gerard and his thermometer, grain samples, and Hebrew-French phrase book, he looked like just another lonely middle-aged Jew, far from home and missing his wife and children. His face was sunburned and peeling; there were broken capillaries, sunburn upon sunburn. Pale smile lines radiated from corners of eyes, corners of mouth. It was a face of hard work and abstract conviction. His family waited on the kibbutz back home. He was doing this service and he would use his pay to buy an earth-mover. In Israel he had built ponds to raise fish—*pisciculture* was a new word to me—refining the techniques taken by Yugoslavs from the ancient Chinese. And now here he was also planting tilapia, the African shmoo-fish, in the streams and ditches, besides constructing a few experimental carp ponds for venturesome Haitian businessmen.

"They are a wonderful people. They are so beautiful. But there are certain problems—" And he shook his head over the difficulties of organizing fish ponds and threading a way through bureaucracies in Haiti. "But they are a beautiful, wonderful people."

He meant the perfume of Haitian women, the great gold hoops of earrings, and the sliding, enticing walk of those women. There were wonderful things in Haiti. A sensual walk served not to clean the ponds, or to keep the spry safe from the voracious frogs, or to feed the grains into the stream at the proper steady rate.

"—a wonderful, wonderful people, anyway. But they don't know anything about fish."

He was lonely and I was married, with small children in the house, and thus he became uncle, grandfather, guide, and patron, in return for a place to sit and talk about Israel. "We can learn from these beautiful, wonderful Haitian people," he said. "They know how to dress so beautiful. They can sit and do nothing and smile so. We need to learn some of that, too."

In the meantime, Monsieur Gerard, his colleague, learned to plant fish in the ditches, flooded fields, and waterways. I traveled with them by jeep into the markets of Les Cayes,

St.-Marc, Jeremie, and up the mountain from Port-au-Prince to Kenscoff—pine and eucalyptus, a sudden spring in the perpetual humid August—and everywhere tilapia could be bought for a few pennies in the marketplace. Tilapia is a stubborn little African fish which grows eagerly in salt, brackish, or fresh water, in ditches, streams, rice fields, ponds, and puddles, breeding handsomely anyplace, provided only that the water remains warm. It had not existed in Haiti; Tal brought it from Africa. Planted occasionally, it grew throughout the island. Tal guessed that the fish, installed near the mouths of streams giving onto the Caribbean, had been carried to the mountains by birds; or perhaps eggs had clung to the birds' wings and then been dropped in mountain sources. The upstream magic of fertility.

We stood in the market at St.-Marc and looked at some cooked fish in a pan. *"Combien?"* I asked.

"Deux cob."

"Qu'est-ce que c'est?"

"Poisson juif."

They had never seen a Jew, but somehow they knew by the *"telejiol"*—telemouth—that this fish was to be called Jewfish. In another village it was called *poisson israélite.* And in another, *poisson Assad*, because it had been found first here on lands belonging to a man named Assad, a Lebanese. The *telejiol* works like magic—but not perfectly.

Tal played with my children, counseled my wife, told us his troubles, and said, "Someday you will visit us on the kibbutz." Amid the drums of voodoo ceremonies, the crazy golden age of Haitian prosperity—generals in Eisenhower jackets tailored in Jamaica, much aid from elsewhere—it seemed odd to remember the nation of Jews far away and for which this man longed. "It is not so much luxury, but it is nice," he said. "If they let us live, you will see swimming, culture, fine things. This could be a beautiful, wonderful country, also."

I took ill with malaria and he sat by my bed. I thought I would die, but he was smiling and I knew I would live.

He told me about the other Israeli in Haiti—Morgen, a tomato farmer. He was a Jew who called himself an Israeli, and therefore Tal considered him what he said he was, though he spoke no Hebrew. He grew tomatoes with cheap Haitian labor. He planned to ship them to Florida. He would get rich on delicious little year-round Haitian tomatoes. He borrowed money and took the required uniformed Haitian partners. They grinned at sharing with him. Sometimes they came to inspect the fields and took a bite from a tomato, and when the juice ran down the lovely front of the Eisenhower combat jacket, an aide ran forward to wipe.

Suddenly there were new taxes. Why new taxes? Morgen wanted to know.

Taxes, everyone knows about Haitian taxes, but Morgen didn't know. It was a game they played with foreign business-men—not Brown & Root, not the big companies from Texas, but with the tasty little innocents like Morgen. Morgen didn't know what he was doing.

However, if he increased the balance of the partnership, an arrangement could be made about the taxes. How to do that? A colonel, squeezing delicously into a tomato, little pink seeds on his chin, suggested that his share be doubled.

"But twice fifty percent is one hundred percent!" cried Morgen.

The colonel made a lightning calculation. "Yess," he said.

"That leaves nothing for me!"

The colonel's lips bubbled fresh tomato juice. He agreed. Yess.

"Impossible, impossible!" Morgen wailed.

"Possible," said the colonel, a resourceful mathematician.

Morgen found himself one midnight being awakened by gentlemen in a police Buick. He finished the night in jail. He passed a few more days in this place. A Haitian jail is as bad as a Syrian one, especially when a man's partner is not only an army colonel, but also a police colonel. A Syrian jail might be worse, but a Haitian jail is bad enough.

Tal found the correct channel for the money and got him out. "Go home, not to America," he said. "Son, you're not a tomato rancher. Don't try to do something you can't, such as raising tomatoes in Haiti."

"I'm not really an Israeli," said Morgen. "It's very complicated."

"Well, be one. It's your last chance. You're no bargain, Morgen."

Tal sat by the bed in which I was recovering from malarial hepatitis, smelling the damp ticking of my mattress, and told me that the poor fellow was just a confused Jew from middle somewhere-else who thought he could purify his soul with tomatoes and dollars. He had a tattoo on his wrist. A survivor, but a war casualty. Tal shook his head mournfully. "The trouble we get into," he said. "In Israel it's different. Different trouble. I don't think we can make anything with Morgen, but he's tired. He thinks all you have to do now is grow the tomatoes. He should go home to rest."

It was tempting to make the Israeli fishing expert the bearer of my hopes for a Jewish hero in life and a Jewish community on earth. And I surrendered to that temptation and hope. Amid the smell of mangoes and woodsmoke, the hot winds off black history, the humid simmering of Port-au-Prince, I had found a few black Roman Catholic voodooesque Jews. The traders of a hundred years ago, a hundred and fifty years ago, yesterday, had wandered so far, trying their luck, and died after planting their brown Cohens, Goldenbergs, Weiners, Levis, Schneiders on this forgotten island. In the mulatto population of Haiti there were also French, Germans, Danes—one family of beautiful coffee-colored girls with Scandinavian faces, finally achieving the smooth tan which Danish women always want—and gloomy Poles from the village of Casals. And Jews. Who? Whose?

Where do I ever find them?

Wherever I am. Within myself.

Where is that?

It was in Haiti just then, amid the descendants of, among others, the gloomy Poles. But also there was the beautiful Dr. Goldenberg, plump, brown, *diplomée* from the Cornell Medical School. "They use make-up," Tal said. "They walk so. They dance so. Our women can learn from them even now," said the man who disseminated the Jewfish. He would have liked his daughters on the kibbutz to learn the secrets of Creole grace from the languorous *doctoresse*, Felice Goldenberg.

To fix in the mind a good man is a difficult task. What do you remember? Kind smiles, a habit of amiable judgment? Heroes make extraordinary sacrifices in moments of danger, but Tal merely took friendship from me and gave his own in return. He was a good man, and what I remember after the fish-farmer's love of fish was his joy when they spawned in a tricky pond. "Look! There will be good spry!" And that he watched the beautiful Haitian girls avidly and in all innocence. The desire to find small perfections in womankind and in nature constituted the hope in his loneliness for country and family.

• • •

The persistence of Jean Berlin, his grin, shrewdness, secret knowledge, his handsome roars of Haitian laughter: "I'm the only one in the family who remembers. Of course, I'm a Catholic like everyone else." Delighted and maliciously elated because of his grandfather from Berlin: "I know, I know anyway."

My friend Cohen, the anti-Semite, who found a business to suit his temperament. He imported Manischewitz Kosher Wine, sweet and thick, and advertised it for Saturday nights. *Kosher* was the magic word he blandished, magic first of all for himself. He understood the Haitian tradition of fear of the white stranger and longing for his potency; the mysteries of the alien people had disturbed his own soul. Fountains of youth and aphrodisiacs are always popular in Latin and Caribbean places. "KOSHER!" screamed the newspaper announcements. The anti-Semite, Cohen, felt pleasure surge through his body at the menace and promise of the Word. He would profit from it. "KOSHER! Guaranteed to be KOSHER! Try it and see! Try it tonight! If it doesn't turn out to be KOSHER, your money back!"

The tailor in Jacmel, with his bad eye and his attendant court of brownish children, squatting in the dust of a dying colonial town, dying forever, dying for many generations, dying forever and persisting in life. He sat by his machine and we groped for our few words of Yiddish and finally spoke French and Creole with each other. Two Jews in Jacmel, finding Creole their common language for saying they have a nostalgia for a town they had never seen—Jerusalem.

• • •

Haiti was a land without Jews, no rabbi, no place of worship, no community, and yet one Jew, Shimon Tal, made it a Jewish place for me. In the cemetery there were Jews buried, with crosses over their graves.

When I recovered from malaria, I wanted to go with Tal to Jacmel to meet old Schneider. "I'm waiting for that," Tal said.

We took a jeep, bucking and churning over the rocky dry streambeds into the isolated village. I asked myself how the squinting Jewish tailor, dry as a pod in the sun, survived that Haitian male vanity which leads every man to seek to be the *coq du village*. Well, for one thing, he seemed to have most of the children of the town. He rode with the vanity. He removed himself into himself, and observed his children, blood of his blood, growing their own souls, compounded of Schneider and of Haiti. And old as he was, teasing with me, he had touched his own balls for luck against the stranger.

Suddenly dust, chickens, speedy black pigs in the road, and the leaning nightmare craziness of Jacmel. I expected to find the tailor sewing in the street, as I had first seen him. But it was an overcast day and maybe he was indoors. *"Où est Monsieur Schneider?"*

"Pas conné," said a child, and ran. I was sure it was one of his sons. He stood as far away as he could, giggling and shouting, *"Pas conné."*

Of course he knew.

"Où est Schneider?"

In his house, open to the street, the sewing machine stood dusty on a base of slats in the corner. He had died and was forgotten—weeks dead. He had died and was not forgotten. There was a ceremony that night for the rest of his soul.

In the *hounfor*, the temple outside town in the brush, an

all-day ceremony was going on, three drummers urging the congregation into a whole series of voodoo possessions by the new god Ibo-Juif. Tal and I joined the stream of communicants. Evidently Ibo-Juif was a happy god. The celebrants were drinking the blood of a bull recently slaughtered, catching the thick flow in pans laid at the slit belly. Gleaming mulatto boys, all named Schneider, danced about us, with firm tiny erections after so much excitement and laughter. It was slaughter and homage for the disappeared tailor from the Ukraine. His Haitian family danced, seeming to climb in the air, hauling invisible ladders after them as they climbed, and only the wife sat exhausted by her weeping in a corner of the zinc-roofed shack. Waves of drumbeats swept over her grief. The boys grabbed their genitals for luck and consolation in the time of the death of their father.

Tal and I stood silent. Then Tal's lips were moving. He ignored the need for ten men, he ignored his own atheism. He was murmuring the prayer for the dead. Later I told him he should have held himself in the groin in that all-purpose Haitian curse, blessing, and reassurance of power in the midst of ultimate powerlessness.

We returned to Port-au-Prince almost without speaking except for the necessary collaboration of the road. I stood in a stream to guide the jeep forward over a mud bank; Tal showed me how to spin a jack tool when a tire blew out in a stretch of dried ruts. By the time we reached the outskirts of the capital—market women, dogs and chickens and pigs in the road, peddlers, the mobs of hungry-eyed children staring with dead sugar stalks in their mouths—we could talk of other things. His family, my family, fishing, the Artibonite dam project which would stand as an uncompleted ruin when the Magloire government fell.

135

"You will visit me at Nir David?" Tal asked. "We have found a Roman mill. Underground waters which was tapped maybe three thousand years ago. Were tapped?"

"Yes."

"You will come to see with your family?"

"I don't know," I said.

He was hugging the wheel of the jeep with both arms. "You are thinking about it?" he said.

"Haiti is enough traveling for a while. The Jews of Haiti are keeping me busy enough."

He looked at me, puzzled, the sweat running in rivulets through the dust on his face, and then realized he knew enough English to understand me correctly. He smiled his broad fish-farmer's smile. Haiti has no Jews.

I learned in Haiti that to be a Jew required nothing at all (I was well equipped with that). And this ignorance led to a powerful understanding, that history really exists and therefore I am a part of it, and there is no oblivion anywhere but in death, no salvation anywhere but on earth. It seemed unfair to abandon lonely men to that lonely place, the kingdom, empire, and republic of Haiti, but fairness played no part in it, for them or for the starved children on the road. That Jews had always been there and left their mark was nevertheless a profound comfort to me. The continuity of suffering is a paradoxical form of reassurance, but it can happen like that anyway. It was possible to survive anyplace; it is necessary to survive somehow.

As Haiti became a land filled with Jews, so my heart was filled with the sense that I was no different from those lonely men who would die on the mountain at the edge of the Forêt des Pins, or had already died in St.-Marc or Jacmel, or in the erosion of time as their sons forgot who their fathers were.

Their sons do not forget; or if they do, nature does not, which shapes them; and if nature does, history finally does not.

Reconciliation also brings practical joys. My rearing, Cleveland and immigrant, would not let me populate Haiti with ghosts and spirits; that would be superstitious and a waste of a good education; but I could remember how my mother always wanted me to be another Jewish doctor, and then contemplate with a various vision, with my mother's passion for medical degrees and my friend Tal's for erotic good sense, the luxurious walk of the mocha-colored *doc-teureuse,* Felice Goldenberg.

When we left Haiti a few weeks later, I had troubles in the customs house with an officer who wanted to put mysterious taxes on our belongings. He was that cool official, known the world over, who makes others sweat. The sun beat down murderously on the zinc roof; fingers turned slimy as I tried to fill out forms; he knew exactly what he wanted and the heat could not touch him. Amid the shouts, groans, and shrieks of stevedores, the dust and reek of the port, he remained calm, wearing military khakis and a khaki tie with a question mark embroidered on it. My wife asked him what was the question, and he answered, "A *blanc* will never know. *Même pas une blanche.*"

He grinned and showed his teeth and his charmed face looked as if it could open up and send the flies reeling in his life's sweet breath. I argued for our rights against the taxes he had invented on the spot, export duties on my own shirts, inspection duties, *impôts de passage.* I called out the names of our friends in the military, in the government. Finally he shrugged and said, "Give me half the tax."

"No, that's ridiculous."

"A third."

"No."

"Then ten dollars," he burst out, "for my time which I have wasted on you! I've got to get something from you now." And he grabbed himself for magic against defeat by a foreigner.

I felt evil myself for beating him down so fast. It was too easy. Yes, I would give him a ten-dollar bribe, and hope that all my suitcases got on board.

It was not difficult to offer him the money. It required no special envelope, slyness, or tact. During my year and a half in Haiti, I had learned the basic techniques. Take money from pocket, hold it between two fingers. Recipient extends palm and pauses a moment submissively. His eyelids fall dreamily. Look nonchalant. Let bill touch hand. Hand closes; the heat of two bodies shimmers invisibly; it is an incomplete communion, celebrated through the intermediary of abstract work and goods in the form of cash.

Tal was there to bid us goodbye, and Captain Prosper said, "That is why I make things so easy for you. Monsieur Tal has brought us the *poisson israélite.*"

"Thank you very much," I said.

"You are also Israelite?"

"He is an Israeli. I'm an American."

"The Republic of Haiti declared war on Germany twenty-four hours before the United States. Good thing you did, however, you North Americans. And the Republic of Haiti voted for Israel in the United Nations—I know my history— though it is said that certain Zionist agents purchased the vote of Haitian diplomats. Alas, the Foreign Service seems to have been corrupt in that period—"

I had heard the story.

He opened the door courteously, and we stepped out of the cookery of the customs shed (zinc roof, heat reflecting crazily, like scooting mites across the eyes), out onto the wharf, where the gang bosses' screams of abuse replaced mechanized loading equipment. Captain Prosper fingered the raised question mark on his tie. "One of our first visitors was a Jew," he said. He grinned happily. "Christophe Colombe." And roared with laughter. The ten-dollar bill stuck out of the pocket of his *veston eisenhower.* "Columbus brought syphilis to the island, destroyed the Carib Indians, and made room for civilized Dahomey people, also Ibos, also Yorubas. Personally, I happen to be descended straight from an Abyssinian prince, and we go back, as you probably know, through Sheba to the King of the Jews."

Probably most people settle for agreeing that Detroit and Port-au-Prince are different cities. They are, I mean, so foreign to each other that you just don't have to keep one in mind at the same time as the other. And that's probably a wise simplification, for it makes the brain warp back upon itself to move from Haitian voodoo, animal sacrifice, and possession by the gods, to General Motors macumba freeway magic.

My first quarrel after leaving Haiti was with a class at Wayne University. I pointed to a Buick advertisement as an example of erotic promises, corrupt poetry, bargains in power smuggled into the salesman's pitch for a mere automobile. "Instant Command?" I asked there near the shadow of the freeway interchange. "Do you really think a new Buick can give you Instant Command?"

The class was boiling and snapping at me. A revolution for principle was ripening in the midst of these strained faces, working out for upward mobility in a commuters' college. They earned their livings with automobiles, they loved cars, they treasured the thought of them. Even accessories were a joy to contemplate—levers, buttons, options, dashboard animals. Their parents worked in the plants and, themselves, they were heading for foremen or offices or sales.

"Instant Command? Like a girl? Step on her gas and away she goes?"

This was un-American. It was un-Detroit. This was some smart-ass professor creep. "That's not the point!" someone yelled. "You're just looking for things!"

I had insulted the fair name of Buick. I was guilty of lèse-Fisher Body and who the hell did I think I was? What right had I to pick at the thing that prevented this place from returning to beaver-blocked swamps? (Only it wouldn't: the debris of Flint and Livonia, River Rouge and Chrysler Assembly, would remain forever, like Mayan ruins or the Kaiser-Frazer chassis dump.)

Ah, that's a lovely quarrel for you. It had a clear pedagogical point, unlike the horrid baiting of family, which goes round and round before it comes out unclear. Assault on fake poetry might be worthy of a man who needs to demolish and build. What was bad for General Motors wasn't good enough. It was better than other quarrels.

These were lively, troubled students, many black, many second-generation and poor, worrying hard, with real problems of connection with the America others had defined. They wanted to know how to get what they were told to get.

Some of them had the glint of doubt in their street-wise eyes and cool faces. They were ready to ask: Why want this? Why not something else? It was a fight all the way, since Detroit was not ready to ask why.

Those were record years in the automobile industry. The Korean War, the baby explosion, freeways and suburbs, and the idea of power and speed all came together nicely for Detroit. So Detroit believed. *Automation* was a new and magic word, dreadful, promising. Detroit still thought a community could be built out of the rewards of assembly lines.

It turned out, after all, that Port-au-Prince and Detroit are not absolutely strange to each other. They both believe in magic, and both go up in rage at the threat of black magic, harmful disruption, doing it another way. I learned that lesson. The brain does warp back upon itself.

My second major quarrel lacked a fine pedagogical point. It was with my wife. It taught no lessons, but it exhausted the spirit. The third one was different, but it was also a continuation of the second. Household equipment was sacrificed to the gods of discord. Dishes—the traditional weapon. Clothes ripped. Satisfying crashes, stains, debris; impulsive destructions. No sweet climax. The fourth quarrel had a different incentive, but it too was a continuation of earlier ones. The fifth the same. The sixth the same. They could no longer be counted. A tribute to human energy: people worn to the nerve could still find strength to make new trouble, trying out possibilities for despair. We restored ourselves as best we could in vague, distracted, anxious insomnias. We spent our strength in swirling, snarling excitements. And then begged each other for respite. Heads down, eyes distant and worried, we asked only love and sought only hatred.

I had married a girl of my own sort, midwestern and Jewish

and a lot of nerves, and now our family was coming apart. Amazingly, I took on a sort of calm as I fell in love with writing; I learned to loaf and laze as I explored this vocation, and our family was coming apart. Surely I cared less about the task of being all things, brother, father, and prince, to this lady. I was no longer a knot of nervous boy, merely resistant to the hostile world. The world seemed to hold lively possibilities for adventure. I was writing a novel about a nervous boy. As I found my place in the world, and what the good fights might be about, my family was coming apart. Sometimes it seemed to make me more nervous than ever not to be nervous. I was more on edge than when I really had the jitters. Sometimes it didn't seem worthwhile to grow out of Cleveland ways. Quitting the childish style made its own sort of childishness, and I ranted and stamped, shouting that I wanted solidarity, trust, and kindness, and therefore I threw food and furniture, too.

The quarrels had no number. They were waves on the ocean, stretching as far as we could see. And yet she and I both sometimes thought we could stand on the beach like kings of old and command the sea to go back. She would be the perfect wife if only I would be the ideal husband. Fair enough, a good deal, but I couldn't live up to the condition. So if our marriage wasn't to be an ideal of heaven, it might be an ideal of hell. There was no further choice to be made, no Instant Command. *That's not the point,* someone said. And someone else said, *You're just looking for things.* And it doesn't matter which one said what.

The time of blame is past. I remember a stifling misery, a choking in the heart, bone aches. Regrets led to vengeance, resolutions to rage. The time of blame was essential. I suppose the lady remembers something similar.

• • •

My Last Two Thousand Years

It was March and there had been a late wet snowfall over Detroit. I came home from a daylong conference—organizing a Humanities program for the teacher's college—to find the thermostat set at eighty. The children were in bed. "I'm cold. I think they're getting colds. They look feverish."

"They're feverish because it's so goddamn hot in here!"

I was removing shoes, socks, shirt. I opened the window and put my head out. Bleakness there: a sick bay inside. An icy wind swept through the house. I shut the window. What if they really were coming down with something?

I went to the refrigerator and made a sandwich and sat down at the table lovingly constructed from a flush door, sanded and buffed by a thoughtful lady who liked working with her hands. I wanted to tell her about my colleague, a Professor of the Philosophy of Education, whose first roman numeral under The Industrial Revolution, Six Credits, was: The Introduction of the Oboe. I valued her laughter, her bright scorn for foolishness. We would compose a little playlet as I relived the meeting of the Committee on the Humanities for the College of Education. Protestantism. The Conquest of the Americas. The Introduction of the Oboe.

She sat down, hands knotted, fingers white, to watch me eat and wait for me to complain again about the heat so the quarrel might continue. Her dark eyes glittered. Try. Try it. Too much heat, right? I bit into lettuce, tomato, roast beef. "Good, good, I was hungry," I said.

"Want some cucumber?"

"I didn't see it."

"There's some in the box. Mayonnaise?"

"No."

"You're worried about getting fat?"

"No."

And we both waited. I might still talk about professors of education. She might still talk about what was not in her mind. We might both of us speak of other things. Not likely, but possible. Whatever disasters overtook us, we might still find a way. Not likely as long as the thermostat was used as an attack weapon. Not likely as long as wary distraction made children of us. Not likely, but possible.

"What happened today?"

"I was going to tell you."

"Then tell me."

Silence. I ate. Crumbs in my throat, sweep pulp of winter tomatoes, effort of eating with dry mouth, constricted heart.

Suddenly there was a heavy *plop* against the window. We both jumped. A snowball had crashed against the pane, thunderously shaking it. "Kids," I said, and sat down.

Then in rapid succession: *plop-plop-plop*, three snowballs shuddering the glass. And I was running down the stairway, barefoot on the wettish carpet, and out onto the street, chasing three boys who saw me and started running; I was barefoot in the snow, and felt as if I were a sleigh flying through the leaden skies of Detroit, and for some reason the three kids stayed together—fear of this madman, surely—and at the next corner they darted nimbly, but I caught the telephone pole and jerked myself around, driving a set of splinters deep into my arm, and I had them by the necks (they were boys of twelve or thirteen) and was bearing them down into the snow ("Mister, mister, don't!") and was rubbing their faces in the abrasive slush, rolling over with them—they were terrified— and I was banging their faces each against the other—"Mister, please don't!"

What the devil was I doing?

I stood up, hoarse and shaking.

"Don't ever again throw snowballs at those windows, hear?"

"Mister, we won't, honest, mister."

"There are babies in there. There's my wife in there."

"We won't, honest, mister! We're sorry. Honest."

"You could break the window on them."

"We're sorry, okay? Please. We're sorry."

I went home in the dusk, feet icy in snow, heart pounding, dizzy, depressed, joyous. No more appetite. No more need to quarrel. Oh, it was time for anger, time to do something, time to admit this rage. Those were unlucky boys of Detroit with their ancient urge to heave wet snowballs at a yellow-lit window where a man and a wife sat silently across their table, looking at each other and waiting while one of them ate.

Choice: to go with nobody.

Or to stay with nobody.

Or to look again.

I chose to look again, a juvenile retracing his steps once more. The humanities organizer had better stop beating up neighborhood kids and the only woman in his life. Better find other enemies, other friends. I think I am a writer, but I'm mostly an unhappy husband. An undiscovered community, regret and memories, children and deeds done wrong, half-worked ideas and pride, old obligations and renewed decisions—what else am I? I had thought to be a Jew, but I am too busy dying. This interruption is my whole life now, and when will my life begin?

In such murky, murky, self-justifying ways I spoke to myself in my half of the bed, and all to one avail: *I'll find a girl who likes me.* Juice and heave together was what I desired to tell me something different about myself and the rest of the world, and to rub my engorged face in the abrasive snow.

It isn't so complicated as it seems to beaten husbands. A girl, this silent wild girl who danced in leotards on the roof of her boarding house, offered to take me to the jazz joints of East Jefferson. We speeded up the ceremonies of courtship. The sweat of love, the stench of cigarets, the heaving cries, tears, and laughter; baths, oil, laziness, delights. A mad girl was cunning sometimes, and abandoned. She made me sore and, for long afternoons, sure. I joined her. I cooled by her side and felt my body and soul knitted together. I didn't have to ask where my soul was; it was joined to someone.

I told myself that this father and husband, teacher, member of a committee on the humanities, mournfully nervous, had a right to seize sweetness when he had none. I had daughters, responsibilities, old worries. I was writing a book. I was quarreling steadily, droningly, with a disappointed wife. I drove my daughters to Palmer Park to feed the ducks. Grinding with effort, I had dinners and evenings with my wife and our friends.

And then Detroit was suddenly beautiful. A certain breeze down red-brick streets, a bowling alley where my heart leapt to meet the girl (a bowling alley in Detroit! with a dark bar), a round head and cool blue eyes, my hundred-dollar 1946 Chevrolet with the glass beginning to frost (what's there to see on a Detroit highway anyway?), a window in the boarding house through which I climbed so as not to be found by the retired music teacher from the public school system who watched over the girl's life. Joy at last. After two children. When I thought it had given me up.

With white knees, pink shoulder blades, a sudden flush of sleek sweat, she swarmed over me, I over her, and then to the bath, and then homeward, with her smell still clinging to me. Freedom from childhood at last. How can I make up to others my discovery of pleasure? What can I do to deserve it? I would no longer oppose the idea that the introduction of the oboe is a vital factor in the Industrial Revolution. But there was even more stubbornness to be softened in me. Responsibility replaces responsibility. Duty replaces duty. Joy replaces sorrow. Grief replaces mourning. Rigors. Regrets. Celebrations.

Things would surely get better, though worse; livelier, though confused. Praise the famous blessings of the oboe.

My wife and I had an audience of parked automobiles, Dynaflow gravestones, curved in stasis against hypothetical winds. Fords, Chevrolets, old Hudsons, a hot-rod Kaiser, a few sporting T-birds stood in irregular ranks about our gesticulating bodies. It was a wide lot alongside a theater. We had left the movie before it was over. There was an actress who reminded my wife of someone we had known, I had known. I had looked at her in a certain way. It was obvious.

Cadillac. GM executive maybe, or a doctor. Looked at whom in what way? In what way? With all the world a misery, why trouble about looks?

Screams like River Rouge Plant lathes in that late winter parking lot, the piles of blackened slush diminishing near the sooty hedges which were there for beautification of the windowless brick walls, cold storage on one side, wide-screen movies on the other; shouts like riveting machines, like acetylene torches, like machinery screeching on the night shift. We were finishing our marriage. We stood amid the parked cars, each decorated with stickers, giving permission to park someplace, with toy rear-window dolls which bobbed in traffic, nodding and nodding, with bronzed baby shoes and charms and souvenirs of Korea or General Patton or Mark Clark. We were sending ourselves out into the night.

147

Nearby there was a ramp. These automobiles nudged each other up the ramp and away after the show, the glacial Great Lakes wind whistling past aerials, and the people comfy within, snug with heater and radio and mate and memories of a nice movie starring that girl who reminded my wife of someone we had known. Their cars gave them power, thrust, and instant command. I had a car. Why not me?

"Get in," I said.

We beat the traffic up the ramp. We drove home in silence. But it was all over.

Since I was teaching at the university, I received permission to move into the boys' dormitory. A man with two children, I dwelled down a corridor filled with shouting kids who snapped towels and heaved notebooks at each other. I was showing my sincere intentions. There were no girls allowed in Webster Hall. I suggested that I would give up the blue-eyed dancer. A Sincere Effort. A token of chagrin. I meant it—to try sacrificing what I thought had proved the world was not all a misery, had saved my life.

I lectured on Tolstoy, Dostoevsky, Proust, and came home to boys in jockey shorts. The blue-eyed dancer packed up for New York. "I know I'm letting you down," I said. "I owe this to my family. I have to do this. I have two children."

"Creep," she said.

"It's something we've never talked about. I've tried to put things into compartments. My family and you. You. I meant what I said to you, but I made promises to someone else. I promised my children a fair deal by having them. It doesn't mean I"—for the first time I used the word —"love you less. I love you. You saved my life. But I've got to give them this. My wife. One last try."

"Well, we're not going to talk about it now," coolly stated

the blue-eyed dancer. My wife had left my clothes in a card-board box on the front porch. The lithe lady was putting her clothes into a duffel bag. "They've accepted me at the Actors' Studio," she said. "I'm also going to take the film course at NYU. I really hope things work out wonderfully for you, Herb. You're a real swell fellow. Go fuck yourself."

It was the longest speech she had ever made in my presence.

At night I drove out alone to the nameless after-hours jazz joint on East Jefferson, sharing the pleasures of jazz with after-hours lovers, and said I liked Kenny Burrell as much as anybody in the house. The house was a smoky frame building with sagging beams, dating from prehistoric Detroit, when Henry the Founder was considered an interloper by the descendants of French trappers and fur traders. It was on a slight rise on the long red-brick street. It was a neighborhood of black and mountain people and I wanted to make it Moe's Main Street in Cleveland, and the Choucoune in Petionville, the Rose Rouge on the rue de Rennes. Elsewheres, dreamy elsewheres. In fact, there was wine in cups and marijuana in the johns, a slow trek of held-breath, bug-eyed smokers pigeon-stepping out. Another time and life and this too would be a dreamy elsewhere.

The dancing lady had introduced me; now I was on my own. I was loyal; I only required company. I was trying; I just needed a place to think. I couldn't sleep. I was lonely. I looked for brothers and sisters everywhere. I already had a wife.

I had a Chevrolet of the first postwar crop. The purplish dawning skies of Detroit—trees, birds in trees—were lovely through the frosted glass of the window and made me think of the French explorers who found this city in swamp and junction of river. Cadillac had seen an Indian standing stock-still, arming his bow. Moments of exaltation and freedom at dawn. Thrilled breathing of blue smoke, and then dawn.

But returned at the still hour of dawn to the dormitory where the boys snored, their fresh lips parted. One or two had stayed up all night to study. The eager beavers heard my footsteps down the hallway.

What the devil kind of life was this?

Lawyers.
Money.
Quarrels.
Police.
Cafeteria friends.
Boyish sex.
Jealousy.
Possessions.
Boredom.
Empty telephone lines. Click.
Changed locks.
Explanations.
Threats.
Nightmares.

Embarking on a voyage into new places, I remembered the past, Cleveland, New York, the war, Paris, Port-au-Prince, but those other matters—family, friends, work—lay sealed off, encapsulated in the heart. They seemed complete in memory, no matter how incomplete in fact. All history came to focus on survival today, where the man who listens patiently or the girl who says, *Well, why not?* is the most vivid creature in the world. I was in this state of emergency and mobilization: What is most important sleeps distant in time, and only the immediate alarm or pleasure can claim any attention. Lies become truth, illusion reality, distraction the only security against the void.

I remembered bicycling down the rue de l'Université in Paris. I remembered the flooding tropical sunsets of Haiti, that sudden cool and ease on Canapé Vert or the hillock of Bourdon—insects, drums—when I embraced my wife and we said that we loved. Forget that. Detroit and divorce time now. No link, no solidarity. So it was with me.

Tears.

Tears.

Tears.

Still, there were times when I knew my life would not end in this vanity and self-pity. I imagined someday telling my life to my daughters so they might understand their own. There were damp dreamy nights when Detroit lay dead and I felt alive in that town. I was alone in my hundred-dollar car, traveling from no-place to no-place in the sleeping city, and all seemed possible despite that all was over. I searched the possibilities of Detroit, magic as all cities are—destruction or the fulfillment of dream. There were strangers waiting. A merest chance might find me death on the highway or the one person I could say everything to. The droplets of rain came from elsewhere to penetrate the haze of the city. I was a stranger and as free as the rain.

And the next day I yawned over a sod-filled playground, with my daughters crying "Push me, push me!" from the swings.

And my wife asking questions, making demands, threatening punishments; and the lawyer telling me, "Just don't discuss it any more, I'm talking with your adversary's lawyer . . ."

I wished to believe in God. I wished to believe in the devil. I wished to blame someone, to sell my soul to someone. I wished to be something other than myself, blaming myself. I wished to belong to something, to belong somewhere. Just when I thought to rescue myself by hatred, I felt pity for the distraught soul who was my adversary.

Death. Despair.

And then the old Chevy wheeling me down to East Jefferson, where Kenny Burrell's guitar made me think of Paris, Haiti, Cleveland, New York, all the possible elsewheres; and alive again, still alive.

Sometimes I strayed into the all-night triple-feature movies on lower Woodward. The streets of Detroit seemed unreal settings for a tawdry war. The back lots of moviemakers were real. The thirty-foot-high heads of stars were a community I could join, along with midnight moviegoers all over the country, insomniacs, mental catastrophes, bad-luck kids, the lost and strayed, the bitterly quarreling, those with no home but the dream of home, no play but the dream of play; those who wanted to love and murder. For ninety-nine cents we enlisted ourselves among giants, in the company of heroes. In the Embassy Theater, after Brando's *The Wild One*, fellows in leather jackets stood at the long mirror in the men's room, admiring thrust of hip, curl of lip, and each one was Marlon, striking against the enemy. The faucets leaked. Former pop and beer found a convincing destiny as piss. The thread that led to the minotaur led here. I was dying. I could tell from the smells all around me.

I wore my wedding ring, not for sentiment but as a magic protection against this wasting. I feared inevitable death if I removed all connection. It was the gold lifebelt which kept me from sinking into the polluted seas in which I swam. It was a connection with my past, with responsibility, with love and duty, with my children; and yes, even with my wife. But I took it off to wash, to work, to sleep. The pressure on my scarred finger made it a burden. And one night I noticed that I had lost it.

Okay, then I'll die. Everybody does.

I was in a bar downtown. It was a muggy Indian summer night. Amid the whine of neon tubes, irritable hum of fluorescent lights, men stood at the rail in attitudes of thought or wary defense. I liked noise, but disliked the impure transmission of electricity. The baseball season on a square of television above the Budweiser sign—blue auras representing men. Little Willie John was singing "Fever" on the jukebox. Deep bass Wurlitzer heartbeat rhythms propelled us through three minutes more of our lives. I searched through my pockets. No wedding ring.

I counted off my fingers and examined each knuckle with care. No wedding ring.

I had no extra fingers in my dormitory room to leave it on. I was blinking at my naked hands. My eyes itched. I had disliked wearing the ring. She had made it for me out of dental gold: how could I refuse her gift? I half-wore it. I almost wore it. Sometimes I wore it. She knew about me. Partly because I didn't like it, she made a shrewd estimate of my commitment to this marriage. And now my eyes stung. I had lost my wedding ring which I treasured so much as the symbol of what I hoped to be, husband and father, member of the wide community of husbands and fathers, devoted birthday-rememberer and PTA goer—a dangerous man in the field of self-pity.

Alone again; war again; and no clarity about what I wanted. Rival echoes fought it out in this cavern. A staccato sportscaster in the box above the bar and the symphonic Wurlitzer in a far corner. Bartenders made change and drinkers drank and it was a ceremony devoted to the easing of confused customers. My heavy-lidded helper wondered why I was so skinny and offered me nourishing boilermakers —"shottinabeer, fifty cents. You're not a born drinker, are you, kid?"

Warty benevolence on his face, bored with drunks, curious to have his boredom confirmed by another familiar history. "Tell me your story, kid, come on, tell Uncle Floyd—" When I looked into his face, mournful swirls of meat, I thought of penitence and penitentiary. All he had to do was wait with me. For those who were guilty without being criminals, this magistrate administered justice, absolution, and hangovers. "—tell Uncle Floyd what she did to you . . ."

"She didn't, I did," I said.

"Yeah, yeah, sure. You think it's your fault—"

"I made a lot of mistakes—"

"Later on you'll figure it out better, kid. Come on, this one's on the house, best thing in the world for you."

"Thanks."

"Part of the whole smear. Now you think it all through more sensibly, you hear me?—Uncle Floyd talking to you now."

My wife. My stepwife. That woman. Nothing to think sensibly. Nothing to think stupidly. Nothing to think at all.

"Now I'll be right back, kid, soon as I take care a some a these other good friends . . ."

I was retreated, retracted, soft with chagrin, given entirely to my dull wits. In other words, feeling sorry for myself. Taking the blame is a means of self-pity, too. I was alone, without my children, with no wife but my nightmare one. I let dismal flow over me.

This civilized activity of self-pollution was interrupted by nature. I went downstairs to the men's room. A cool chap in gray flannel, but with a western shirt, pointy flaps on the pockets, was lounging and waiting for me there, and then he said—I hadn't heard this invitation in years—"Hey, how's about it?"

He had that smile of the man at the Apollo in New York.

He was breathing like Fred O'Shea in Lakewood, Ohio.

Mr. Fergus in need.

This man was in need, but he gazed at my mouth and eyes as if he recognized me, knew me well, as if I were the stranger and compatriot he had been hunting up and down Woodward Avenue. He was suave, as if he felt my appetite before I did. He had a natty look of hungry confidence.

How can he tell I'm in trouble?

He didn't know me, but he knew something about me. He thought I was greedy. He would gobble me up.

Ah, nonsense. He didn't know. Not that trouble.

I hurried up the stairway without discussing it with him. I was not his kin. But in weakness, want, self-pity, and indecision, I must have smelled like kin to him, punk and fireworks, available fun.

I moved out of the dormitory. Dormitory life proved nothing to anyone. I began haunting my friends' houses at dinnertime. I practiced hanging out in places. I took my children to parks, to restaurants, to feed the ducks, to feed themselves. I grew weary of telling my sad story to friends, but if anyone stirred the rubble, I was refreshed. The story smoldered. It flared anew.

"Oh, you're that rat," said a stranger to whom I was introduced at a Thanksgiving dinner.

Someone else was telling a version of the story, too.

My brother took me into his life. Others carried the burden. It was like the war, a continuation of adolescence by different means. In crisis, I returned to boyhood. I had dates. If I hadn't lost my wedding ring, I would remove it to seek my fortune. The father of a schoolteacher greeted me cautiously, keeping his place with a finger in the Sunday magazine of the Detroit *News*: "Uh, how much better off is a college teacher? I mean, I know what my daughter makes teaching school, can a college professor do so much better?"

He didn't know I had children and a wife. I rubbed my scarred finger to get the circulation moving. He was reading *This Week* in order to understand the modern world.

"A college teacher doesn't necessarily do so much better, sir."

Sometimes the day began with a girl and then continued with my daughters. Confusion and fatigue. Sometimes the day began with my daughters, and then continued after a shower with a new girl. Fatigue and confusion and a haste to catch up with pleasure. There had been that lady with whom I listened to Kenny Burrell in an after-hours place on East Jefferson. And those two children with whom I fed the ducks in Palmer Park. Crackling nerves took the place of both pleasure and happiness.

On a crowded Saturday afternoon I drove up to an ice cream shop to buy cones for the children. "You wait here, I'll be right back," I said, running in for the ice cream.

In a few minutes, when I returned to the car, Ann and Judy had red, contorted faces, and they were looking bereft into each other's eyes and howling, the tears flooding their cheeks, and I hugged and hugged them, trying to calm them. "What's the matter? What's the matter?"

"We thought you weren't coming back!"

"But I said I was just going in to get the ice cream."

"You're not coming back, Daddy, you're not coming back."

• • •

A colleague, Hank McCann, invited me to dinner with my daughters. "That weak-minded cat of ours, you know, the cat's had a litter." Wouldn't they like to see the kittens?

With his wife, Elizabeth, their five children, a house in the Polish enclave of Hamtramck, a marriage, Hank said he was ready for something more. He drank. He suffered. He said he envied my freedom. He said the something more he was ready for was the sports car menopause, but drinking would take care of it.

Elizabeth took care of him, the children, their life together. His face was covered with eruptions, as if he had been drinking bad water, eruptions upon eruptions, and together with his stringy skinniness, he had something of the look of a crazed Army misfit—a cook's helper in charge of K.P. His voice rose in shrieks when he was excited, and fell to a hoarse whisper when he was easier with the world. He admired my old Army buddy, the poet Morgan Delaney. He did Melville and Mark Twain, and argued that American literature is an account of rage and madness, and listed his own shrill laughter as a critical contribution to the mainstream. Ahab and Nigger Jim and Hank McCann were the great humorous American characters.

My daughters watched me warily as I drove. "Be careful, Dad. Mom said we should be careful with you."

Nervously I ran my hand through my hair. "Why?"

"Mom said we should tell you to drive carefully."

"Oh."

"Why did you touch your hair like that?"

"I don't know, I just did it."

"You're ascared of getting bald!"

The two of them were huddled on the back seat. I could see them in the rear-view mirror, slyly watching me. "Because I touched my hair? No, I was just pushing it out of my face."

"Ascared, ascared! Baldy, baldy!"

"Don't be silly. Do I look bald to you?"

"No, not yet, but you're ascared. Mom says—"

"Now stop that."

"See, you're ascared. But it's not so terrible to be bald. Mom has a friend who's bald."

"Of course. It's nothing to be bald." Baldness is not a mutilation, Aristotle says in *Metaphysics*.

"Mom has a *very good bald friend,* Dad."

"But I'm not."

"Then why are you arguing, Dad? You *think* you're getting bald."

"I do not. You brought it up."

"You touched your hair. Ascared, Dad! Baldy, baldy!"

I drove in furious silence. Said the correct words to myself. Frightened, worried, scared. Not ascared. Asked, "Do you want to go home?"

One of them spoke coldly: "You said we were invited to dinner and see the kittens. Do you prefer to take us home instead?"

"Mom has a very good bald friend, Dad."

"I heard that already."

"Is it boring, Daddy?"

They were united. They would not make it easy for me. I tried to think: They're bullying me out of despair. If I'm angry, if I stop the car and slap at them, if I take them home now, I'll only confirm their despair. But also I must find a way to be firm with them. Haunted by my own children, I remembered being chased by the kids of Lakewood, told I was a Jew and a Christ-killer; and yes, I was a Jew but not a Christ-killer and it couldn't be explained. When a man is ascared, all the old fears rise up. But these were my own daughters.

"Daddy, you say you're not, but *we* think you're getting bald."

"I don't think so." Such calm! "It's not in our family."

"Then why are you arguing?"

"I'm not. You brought it up again."

"Because you touched your hair again, Daddy."

"See, you're worried about it." Her sister confirmed the conclusion.

"No, not really."

"No, not really. Not really no now. No really not now. Now you're angry. Look, we can tell when you're angry, there's that thing you do—"

"I wish you wouldn't nag at me."

"Look, he's hurt. He makes that funny mouth. He's not so angry, but he's hurt. Look, he's getting angry, too."

Red light. Green light. Slow lane of traffic. Detroit drivers celebrating Sunday by driving slowly.

"Do you want to go home?"

"Okay, take us home to Mom. Drive carefully, Daddy. Hey, we're not going to have any fun anyway. Just because he's getting bald, he doesn't like us any more."

Her sister whispered something, and then she said, "You said we were invited to dinner and see the kittens. You promised."

They were waiting to see if I would pull into the gas station and turn around. Through the rear-view mirror I could see these children huddled on the seat, silently watching. They saw a hulk of man, shaggy hair, a neck that must have looked strangely old and weathered, and they were surrounded by machinery. And it was easy to cause promises to be broken.

The father of these two girls, Baldy for short, had the

shakes. He needed the warmth of a home, a mother, some-one's mother, good friends. Hank giggled a lot, but he was my friend, or I wanted him to be, and he would listen. We parked in the driveway near the little house. Elizabeth said, "The children down in the basement, you can play down there. The grownups stay here, I'm going to make tea."

"Do I have to stay, Mommy?" said Hank in a piping voice. He had a fierce high-pitched giggle.

The children clattered down the stairway. Mine too. What a relief. Hank went with them.

"I'm so glad you came," Elizabeth said. "I've been wanting to talk to you about something." She shut the door to the basement. The shouts of Hank and children were suddenly muffled. "I'm in such trouble, Herb."

Before she put on the teapot we had a ladylike, gentle-manly drink. She had five children. I had two. I had lost a wife. Her husband was an ill child. That made six for Eliza-beth. He was downstairs with the new kittens near the coal chute and the furnace. Along with the muffled sounds of shouting, the pounding of feet and running and yelling, the faint smell of coal smoke in the house, there was something new between us: flirtation. In our misery, we were playing at a new game for both of us.

Her husband drank too much. He was erratic. She feared him.

Well, I had different complaints about my wife. I said we probably each of us saw them worse than they really were.

"Not me," said Elizabeth with New England severity and firmness. "I'm sure I still see him better than he is."

"Elizabeth. He's my friend."

She looked at me with wild eyes. "He's not!"—an abrupt inky blackness. "Oh dear, I don't mean that. I mean he's not a friend to himself or anyone."

I must have shrugged.

"I envy you," she said. "With you it's, well, dislike, or hatred, or something nice like that. In this house it's madness. Don't twitch like that, Herb."

"I'm sorry." But what I was thinking was: Anyway, he likes to play like a pal downstairs in the basement with the children.

"You trust him," she said.

"Shouldn't I?"

"No."

"No?"

"You shouldn't," she said. "He believes what he reads. Mark Twain and Melville and whoever else has theories. The cat just had kittens."

"Is that some kind of code?"

"No. Cat, birth, kittens."

"Righto. Am I stupid? Twain and Melville aren't the most theoretical writers. He's pretty safe from theory in the American novel."

"Well, wait," she said. "He reads Henry James, too."

"I don't care if he reads Edith Wharton, Elizabeth. No skin off my tail. What the devil's the matter with you?"

No more waiting. Screams and shrieks from the cellar. Elizabeth knew the way, it was her house, but somehow I was ahead of her, running down the wooden stairs. Hank was standing at the open grate with a basket under his arm. The children were in a seminar circle about him, their mouths open, the high-pitched wail tumbling in a steady stream over their vibrating tongues. The glow of bituminous fire on Hank's face gave him the smiley pinkness of a healthy boy. A mild crackling peep, a strong meat smell, and spitting tufts of fur.

The basket was empty except for shreds of newspaper.

"Wait!" he said, holding up his hand to me. "Don't get sore, pal. Have you read Unamuno? The tragic sense of life? They have to learn. On the farm, on the frontier it's easier for kids. I wanted my children to learn, too, and it's sure time for yours." He reached into the basket and threw a handful of paper into the furnace. "Dust unto dust, and unto dust be thy destiny."

And then I hit him. And at that moment my daughters stopped weeping.

In Manhattan, in the community of girls and the commerce of culture, I might continue at age thirty-two the youth which had been interrupted by nearly ten years of marriage. What is the proper labor of a man in dispersion? New York was the place for that question, for ways to answer and not answer it. This was my season for rambunctious energy after hurt and convalescence. The West Side of Manhattan had room for another fury. It hummed with secrets like a strange clanking forest, subways, construction, destruction, fierce animal kids and browsing herds of wandering elders, a jungle outside and, within, the snug cell of my retreat near a cooing nest of elevators.

I took lodging in a furnished maid's quarters, with Goodwill end tables and a tufted green couch that heaved and groaned like some ancient domestic beast when I sat on it.

The widow whose apartment it was, West End Avenue and 101st Street, sometimes left fried potatoes wrapped in newspaper at my door to indicate that her will toward me was of the highest and best. She left me undisturbed in my two nervous domestic activities, bringing girls home and running my writing factory.

The girls were a function of some pay-me-back overload. I had missed out on the fun. I was catching up and taking revenge. I'm not proud of it. I was impure.

The factory was to support my daughters in Detroit: to make the profession of writing do a work it was not made for. Once I dreamily gave myself to words. Now the dreamy words had to pay the price of divorce. Well, no complaint. It was better than not paying the price.

George Wiswell, editor of *Nugget,* a *Playboy* imitator, asked me to interview Vikki Duggan, the famous starlet, who had invented something new in late-Eisenhower fashion—a backless dress with reverse cleavage. *Nugget* would pay for lunch at the Stork Club (Vikki liked that). *Nugget* wanted something sharp and different. *Nugget* would let me use a pseudonym.

I felt like a boy offered a strange pudding, Vikki Duggan and the Stork Club, raisins and suet and dreams of delightful corruption. It was a long step from organizing a curriculum in the humanities for a teachers' college in Detroit. I would pick up the lady in a taxi at her apartment. This seemed realer life than the Industrial Revolution and subhead roman numeral one, The Introduction of the Oboe, even though that other real life was conducted under my own name. Perhaps true love might blossom between the girl of the season and the pseudonymous biographer for *Nugget.* She might never before have met a man who truly understood her. I was new to New York.

I was standing at her door, absorbing the meaning and truth of Vikki Duggan through my every pore. I was busy forgetting what I taught about Helen, Menelaus, and Paris in the Wayne University College of Education humanities program.

"Yes, I rather"—did she really say "rahther"?—"like the Stork."

"Shall we?" I asked.

We should, she seemed to think, picking up her purse. She was a slender light dark thin plump girl. Oh, she was a lovely sliver of sexual invitation—who needs exact dimensions, weights, and colors? I was blinded just by the way she tilted her little chin. But it was my job for *Nugget* to think about her, and therefore think I did. With horn-rimmed glasses, I decided, she could become a beauty to equal the darlings of the humanities tradition. Horn-rimmed glasses would add a look of intelligence to the North New Jersey Girls Roller-Skating champ. Already I had found my line for the *Nugget* text: wit, poetry, and this wild strangeness in the soul of a roller-skating starlet whose chief adult renown until she met me was for the cut of her dress behind.

We hummed along in a taxi, the driver sneaking looks in his mirror. I was proud to be her pseudonymous escort.

Carrying a spiral notebook marked Wayne University because I remained a serious scholar, with high commitment to learning, only trying to support my children through a difficult divorce, I wasn't one of those make-out journalist creeps who write interviews with starlets under their own names. I used a fake name, the hero of my satirical first novel, Reuben Flair. But when she took satirical Reuben Flair's arm, Herbert Gold's dead-earnest heart thumped.

Miss Duggan—it's from the French, "Du Gant," she explained—sighed and scrunched down in her seat as we passed a construction project. On her difficult journey through life she had to summon taxis and hide like this, because otherwise the death of high-rise construction workers lay on her conscience. They fell like dizzy flies off scaffoldings when she passed; she would never forgive herself.

For other people, less lovely people, the journey through life is difficult in other ways.

The cabby, participating fully in our conversation, said, "Me too, I like to shit when I saw you. I nearly hit that truck, and I got the safety award two years going."

"Thank you very much for that little tribute," stated Miss Du Gant.

Humble, muted, and shy, he passed back a tablet with a few other autographs on it. "Famous people I drove in my hack," he explained. "Sign something affectionate."

She gave it thought, then wrote in a roundish scrawl: To a real person Vikki Duggan.

At the stoplight he stared at the signature with its circled *i*'s. "Who's that?" he asked, lips rehearsing the letters and making a little pout when he came to the circled *i*'s. "Never heard of you, miss, I'm sorry, but you in a show?"

We sat in a corner of the Stork Club and Miss Duggan told me all her secrets, such as that she wrote poetry, like Jayne Mansfield; liked men, like Marilyn Monroe; and wanted to be a great actress, like, um, the great actresses of the past. Not just a sex goddess. She was under contract to John Wayne Productions to be an *actress*. She had a good part coming— John Wayne's secretary, she thought it was. She looked hurt when I mentioned the North New Jersey Girls Roller-Skating championship. "I really love poetry, that's my first love," she said. She hated to see the construction men perish off the scaffolding as she passed. "I love the game of chess—my true first love, Herb." I wondered what the devil I was doing to earn a few hundred dollars. At least Miss Du Gant enjoyed the con she was giving out, and I only told myself I liked it.

Just living from day to day seemed like a much more demanding class assignment than writing, and the hard work of writing—was it hard work? I made it desperately easy work —was done in an exhausting state of somnambulism, images brooding in head all the time and then rushed onto paper while my head spun around; the body a bit behind the head; the head-and-heart's dreaming inviolate, it seemed, despite the soiling exigencies of surviving day to day. I was wrong about that. Not inviolate.

My landlady, hiding behind the door, listened to the typewriter jump on her Goodwill table. What the devil kind of factory am I? My shoulders hurt after I hit the machine as if it were throwing rivets onto steel.

I had recently published a novel, *The Man Who Was Not with It*, destined, of course, to change the world this time and put my picture on the five-cent stamp. I had made the real unreal and the unreal real. Amid the Ike doldrums and the new beatnik mongering of self, I committed an act of magic —drawing the meaning of life out of the jabber of those carnival wildballs I loved in my adolescence and still love. Well, it got some good reviews and some bad ones. First I suffered the paranoia of I-Wrote-a-Book disease, and then the thought: *Is this all? Is this what it's about?* I wrote a book and it was published and it speaks to some and not to others—is that all there is?

Brood with buzzing head over coffee, and then, like a spider, spin a web from my own body that might catch a few flies?

Not a proper history for a man and a member of the community of men. This work I do, these dreams I have, should not define a life. I knew I had more to do on earth, but for the moment, I defined the *more* as girls for my soul and money for my obligations. Of such curious substances Manhattan helped me to define reality. It too is a spider. I'll not apologize too many times. Since marriage and the conjugal life did not make the community I sought, then the nervous gaming of ambition and pleasure in Manhattan would be my alternate fate. So I let it seem. Greedily I embraced the competition and fun and stroking of the self which I had glimpsed from my miseries as a spouse. What joy not to be in hot little rooms with a wife, rending and being rent! What release to make my own silences! I was unready for possibilities other than varieties of isolation. I thought these were the options of pain and liberation.

For the moment I found my way by an aggravation of energy, spattering out hashmeat articles and heartfelt horror stories. Down and Out in Paris and Shaker Heights. Disc jockey ideals. Hopped-up refugees from the GI Bill. Then I began a novel, *Salt,* about the worn-out young men of New York—bachelor masturbators and divorced night-wanderers and their girl-fodder. They were the ones who mortgaged love and sold liens on their desires. A stockbroker, an advertising copy writer, a Village chick who decorated fashion windows. It was too close for mere discomfort; I came to love them. Their greed was mine.

I used words, the common property of everybody, and a somewhat debased property now, to appeal one more time to the private language of dream and unknown tradition in each reader; and not simply to validate his own fantasies, but to lead him to something new for him and also for me: a discovery of my own myth through words uttered already countless times in history and borrowed from the common store. In this triangulation of discovery, from language to other to writer, and back around again and again, is produced novelty, art, and finally that highest desire, community among men. It is the way creation finds its way back to the deepest meaning of religion. We touch others responsibly and with risk; *communicate*, putting all of us together in danger; *community*, meaning we share our fate.

And I sought these things while playing the nervous games of the time. During my hours of work I lived with this hope. They were real people, my brothers and sisters, discovering their destiny in my furnished flat as I made marks about them in spiral notebooks. The rest of the days and nights I smiled among the speedy psychopathic charmers of Manhattan, maladapted and secretly okay, just making out fine.

I wrote to my daughters, wondered if they received my letters, and then, like a spoiled brat myself (no reply), fretted at the strength they drew from me, strength I needed to survive in this distant city; assigning blame for their failure to reply, their puzzled hurt at my absence and silence, I wanted to kill; and then a glimpse of a woman with a child on Riverside Drive, and I fell in love upon sight with both child and unknown mother; and then telephoned to say I was leaving right now for Detroit, where I invariably caught the flu and two weeks later had a scarring fever blister (herpes dwelled in the same spot on my lip, a nest of virus, there's a scar forever).

I resented the claim on me. I adored them. I was responsible for their fate. I wished I could be free of claims. I did the work of the world to get the money demanded for them. I couldn't blame them, no matter what. I had a powering fury to write for them, even to explain to them. I was alone in my bondage, it seemed, despite all the East and West Side fathers taking their children to Disney matinees—no community in this collection of stony escorts with wild charges.

Arrangements were made for my daughters to stay with

me in New York. Rights of Visitation. The dangers of flight, train, and escorts were all negotiated with the help of stubbornness and insistence. Ann said about my apartment: "It's so small." And then Judy: "But we like your so small house, Daddy." Empire State Building, Automat, Statue of Liberty, and the Cloisters. The house they liked was my factory. I didn't really live in it. I lay awake in the dark, comforted by the echo of those words. *Daddy . . . I like your so small house.*

The city was full of writers who began their lives full of doubts about themselves and others. They resolved the problem by continuing to mistrust others, but by learning to love themselves with extraordinary passion in order to make up for the faults of the world. They burned with tenderness for the only pure heart in town. In their books they spoke of love, faith, generosity, and trust, fractioning off pieces of self-devoted sweetness, but it was their own hurt, the healing of their own hurt, themselves as doctors to themselves, for whom they were writing prescriptions.

All love begins with self-love, we are told by the human heart experts, pediatrics division; true enough, I suppose; but somehow we are supposed to move on from childish self-love and arrive at the love of others as ourselves. The professional charmers settle for seeming. The witty, cynical, or deeply pressured ones found styles—hipness, elegance, violence—to signal the presence of the lack. They were serious; therefore they settled for evasion and fame.

The serious writers.

The trivial ones were just trying to make out. The pretentious ones were trying to sell off pieces of the serious ones. The sickness of Grub Street in the metropolis came partly because so many suddenly got what they wanted; it was the beginning of boom times for writers (prizes, advances, fellowships, money). They were stuck with what they craved. Writers from Brooklyn, Texas, or Chicago were introduced to the style of the steamed-clam eaters, men like Morgan Delaney's father, now directors of foundations, shifting in and out of tax-exempt operations, bringing novelists and poets into clubs with smiling bartenders and Christmas funds, memberships passed on through the male line, wives welcome in the downstairs bar. "Well, it's a nice place to meet, a little refuge from the city. Now tell me: your new book—"

It's about Duluth. It's about the Industrial Triangle. It's about the decay of the Inner City.

"Would it profit from being written, say, in the Villa Castiglione? Would you learn from visits to Silone, Sartre, and the Old Vic?"

And as in all boom times, in basements nearby, others waited in anguish for some of the success of which they had heard rumors to trickle down. They choked on their bile, they cracked up, they awaited their turn. In the meantime, they listened to the geniuses of the season telling about the apocalypse, David, on talk shows: "In my new book, David, where I rip open the existential malaise of my generation, David—"

That notorious Jewish control of literary Manhattan—that is, Dwight MacDonald, Robert Lowell, Mary McCarthy, the daily book reviewers, Norman Cousins of the *Saturday Review* and Francis Brown of the *New York Times*, all the Manhattan literary tribes—nourished the paranoia of writers as other myths nourished other paranoias. My friend Sam McGraw couldn't get his books taken by a hardcover publisher. He published paperback original sex novels and elegant little stories in college quarterlies. Twice a year, finishing one of the sex novels with which he supported his family, he would throw up, drink himself back into debt, and curse the Jews. Twice a year we became enemies, but I said to myself he was merely mad, not my foe. It was a spasm that lasted a few weeks, like the Haitian carnival, and when it was over that year, I introduced him to an editor who took him to lunch at the Fontana di Trevi. Sam was wan, wry, poetic, exhausted. He hadn't been able to hold anything on his stomach. I waited nervously for the news. The editor offered him a contract, thereby proving that he was free to write without Semitic persecution. "You see!" he cried accusingly.

"But he"—that editor—"is not a Jew." And Little, Brown is a nicely Boston large publisher.

He waggled a finger at my nose. "But I had to have you," he said.

Illusion is what everybody knows. And yes, anyway, there really are Jews in publishing, and I too felt like an outsider. It was not a Jewish world. It was a confused hierarchy of business, charm, and con. There were many Jews. It was the Diaspora.

Santha Rama Rau and I made broadcasts together. George P. Elliott and I appeared like Mutt and Jeff at college short-story convocations, or sometimes I might be paired with James Baldwin, or if they wanted a woman, with Anne Sexton. Once I received an invitation from a midwestern Catholic university, stating that they were inviting speakers representing "the four major religions, Catholic, Protestant, Jewish, and Negro." Ralph Ellison represented the Negro religion. This being the way of the world, I saw no reason why I shouldn't try to stand with my brothers and say only, I'm not from New York. I don't pray very often. I am ignorant of my history. But Jews want salvation, too.

The mysterious Jewish penetration of Manhattan literary life merely meant that there were a lot of Jews, and a lot of

Herbert Gold

everything, but the places which published me in those days
—the Atlantic–Little, Brown, which was doing my books, and
Hudson Review and *Playboy,* which were publishing my
stories—were not considered Jewish even by the paranoids.
Oh, was the answer in colleges when they wanted to know
about that Establishment. Then I must be the House Jew.
Was there something missing in me that I wasn't a part of the
classical *Partisan Review–Commentary* team? Well, sometimes I wrote for them, too. But allegiances are not formed
along the simple lines of Jew and non-Jew, no matter how
simple it may seem to those alternately heated and chilled by
paranoia.

In the rising flood of conquest and gaming, I felt the powers of the world as false to nature. It didn't make me unwilling to play for those powers. There was much time to fill.
Since there was a game, I joined it. It was only a game, and
gradually it filled my life. I confused power over women with
the real power over myself. I cared not so much for the
world. The community which I had sought receded into dim-
ness. The Manhattan of my student days was a village on
Morningside Heights; the Manhattan of careering was a jungle game preserve in which I stalked Miss Right, all of us
ready to stab her in the heart if we had the bad luck to find
her. At first I made sure to find nothing but Miss Wrong. I
courted a solemn intellectual model who wrote for *Common-
weal* and hated to crack her face for laughter. I pounded in
vain. My jokes slipped off the impervious eggshell skin which
seamlessly covered her perfect bones. I had to listen to talk
about Merleau-Ponty, existential psychoanalysis, and the failure of the Worker Priests. However, when time came to say
goodnight, she remembered the entertaining moments, she
did a wonderful three-octave falling run of laughter, she
added up the evening's wit and paid the check all at once,

heeheehee, hahahaha, doing a quick sum of modern
womanly appreciation, oh hee, oh ha, trilling all the way
down to the final *envoi*, hand on doorknob, me not invited
in to muss that Hollins College hair, scrape that Villa Mercedi
skin: "Herb, you're so amusing. You're delightful."

"But."

"But I'm a little distrait tonight. But you're really a tremendous personality."

Gradually, since the town is made for erotic gaming, I
learned the rules of the hunt. I had to find my own special
talent after so many wasted years as student, soldier, husband
and father, fanatic writer, untremendous personality. I
learned to take ladies out of their usual run, as if they were
animals whom I first needed to disorient. I brought them to
the Village, where I fancied myself a king of the jungle, and
this meant to eat in dark downstairs Italian restaurants and
stroll streets where outdoor markets had sprawled just yesterday, my mouth working, my want showing, my arrogance
unnecessary (they knew me), until either full of sympathy or
foolishness or both, they said, "What do you want?"

"Back to my place."

"Okay, okay, why didn't you just say that?"

Nervous time in Manhattan. Sometimes the girl paused at
the door when her place was closer or she needed her equipment for getting to bed or getting to work in the morning,
and she handed me the key, though she knew how it worked
better than I, and watched, humming softly, as I tried to fit
it into the lock. I succeeded eventually, and fumbled better
with practice. "It's so symbolic it kills me," a slender New
York correspondent for a London magazine told me, "but I
can't help it, I like the man to open the door for me, even if
it's my own door."

"I don't mind how symbolic," I said.

"But you're the novelist, aren't you? Doesn't symbolism strike a responsive chord?"

I met a girl who had lent her automobile to her previous lover. She was having trouble getting it back, and so I found myself in emissary clothes, going to collect the car. I thought: What kind of man takes a Studebaker from a lady?

Then I was planning to visit my daughters in Detroit, and she said, "Why don't you use the car?"

Halfway across Pennsylvania on the turnpike, the healthy old Studebaker convertible rattling beneath my feet, a delicious pug designed by Raymond Loewy, I suddenly thought: My God, I've done the same thing! She's given me her car!

I returned it when I came back. "Aw, keep it," she said. "No." "You deserve it," she said, "he'd never have given it back." "No." "Aw, don't you like me?"

"No," I said, "I don't want the car. Yes, I like you."

But I was afraid of being gobbled up, and when it turned out that her economy required offering me a combination of herself and her extra wheels, I decided to continue life as a frequent pedestrian.

When there is no job to be done but the one in your head, it's easy to drift down the evenings, coasting where smoky Manhattan leads. I sat in a book-spattered apartment near Carnegie Hall, the neon outside changing the colors of the curtains (it was a delicatessen sign) while a group of fretful bachelors discussed John Foster Dulles and our former wives, and then, aroused by anxiety and our own talk, we split to hunt up the girls whose names were inscribed in our black address books. Each of us had a girl or two whom we could call late in the evening and just say (poor thing), "I'll be right over."

There were other girls with whom we made variant bargains.

There was one who sought a bargain with me. "Look, I know how you feel about me. But let's make a deal. Once in a while, if I can't sleep, I can call you, okay? And if you can't sleep, if you get the night frights, you know? Anytime you want, anything you want, you call me and come over, okay?"

Claudia furnished her apartment to look like a New Orleans brothel. Teakwood lamps, a chandelier with candlewick bulbs, white fur rugs skinned from wild orlons. She had many-colored telephones. She used ceiling mirrors. She made nearly a thousand dollars a week as a clothing designer. She had a maid whom she proudly described as a call girl's maid. Both her parents were doctors. She was part Spanish and looked like an Inca princess, and dressed for that look—beads, stones, and hand-dyed fabrics. She had graduated summa cum laude from Bryn Mawr. The benefits of tens of thousands of dollars of tooth-straightening, piano lessons, riding and tennis lessons, European trips, schools in Italy and Switzerland, had finally created a girl who said, "Look, we have a deal. I never sleep. Just call, please, I don't care what time it is. I've got some tricks I bet you never tried. It's not love, pal, just insomnia."

She had been married twice. She killed herself at twenty-eight because that was getting a little old for a girl in Manhattan.

All these abstract ladies. I might have rolled up the bits and pieces of girls, as the saying goes, into One Big Girl. A lady who specialized in special things and I saw the whites of her eyes like gibbous moons rolling up. A lady whose kittens jumped on my back in counter-phobic rhythm, putting the fear of sudden death on me. *No cats!* became a condition for true love—a dream princess who kept no cats. Two wives who grabbed and dodged in alcoholic moments, and though I didn't play the mustachioed role assigned by French farce, they both convinced their husbands I had betrayed them. How can you say to a suffering man, "No matter what you think, I didn't. She seemed to want to, but I didn't." Somehow that's not nice for anybody concerned. And a nice sharp copy writer, Catholic and thin, Irish, decided I was the one to initiate her into Manhattan—she was from Trenton and some Sacred Heart or other—and she wept so much into my pillow, just with the thought, that I didn't do a thing to her body, got her a cab home, and threw out the soaked pillow, wet and salty as a Jersey marsh. Hell, the thought was hers, not mine. She needed a Jew for this first service.

My girl lived on the East Side and I lived on options. My girl lived in the Village and I lived on advances. I lived on Waverly Place and my new girl just lived from day to day, too.

The chickies.

My spade friend LaRue and I sat like returned pilots after our missions, eating apple pie and ice cream at O. Henry's on Sixth Avenue.

"How was yours?"

"Okay, A pretty good painter. But she said she only paints what her gallery tells her to paint. That's what they're doing now, she says."

"Um."

"Yours? How'd you do?"

"Okay, strong legs. I like strong legs."

"Dancer's legs? Not so muscled is better, but you know, firm is what I like, too."

"Glad to hear your opinion, buddy. Your opinion is like my opinion."

We were sexist pigs; that is, lonely floaters on the sea. We looked for a community of shared girls. We sought pride and fellowship through the bodies of women. We sought revenge against women through revenge against women. We looked for occasions for heroism and to test ourselves to the limit. We settled for less. We made jokes. We told tales.

My breakfast place on Sixth Avenue gave me eggs and toast and coffee and a small o-j for some bargain price that ended in 9—29, 39, or 59 cents—as the inflation altered values in seven-to-eleven specials. Jim's was a morning rendezvous for the nice neighborhood pederasts, who reported to Jimmy-behind-the-counter on their missions of the night before, as if he were placing bomb pins on the map. "Who did? You did? *He* did?" he asked. "Beautiful, baby! *Where?*" I sat there, continuing my education and being awakened, a double task, waiting till the coffee took hold and I could go upstairs to the typewriter, and hearing someone say, "Well, that's my opinion about that bitch, too," and then I thought: They're using the same language as LaRue and me last night. Vanity. They're lying down with their four paws in the air and stroking their little bellies, just like LaRue and me.

LaRue and I and our kind were living a desolate rhapsody of girls, a one-man opera, with the protagonist standing in front of a backdrop curtain depicting the musical skyline of Manhattan, singing his overflowing heart out in self-indulgent tenor quavering before an audience of mirrors. What we heard was something different—the howl and snarl of the wolf. What a live audience would have noticed was steam on the mirrors, a silent dappling of moisture.

None the less, LaRue and I were different from my friends, the breakfast pederasts, at Jimmy's. We were brothers, but moving in different directions. Finally conquest and the worship of self was not the limit of possibility. The choice of girls —though we thought they were merely the objects of our choice—drove us toward deeper decisions. We ridiculed our young chickies, saying they flunked the Trotsky Test—

"Who was Trotsky?"

"A Russian writer? Some writer?"

—or thought the Spanish Civil War took place a hundred years ago, or believed the world would know peace once every black man was married to a white woman, or looked puzzled or anxious when asked to define "xenophobia."

"English was my best subject." she would say, "but I always liked reading. And when I met the writer-in-residence spring quarter, I just knew I made a mistake not to take more English."

LaRue liked southern girls. I had no particular preference.

The girls newly discovering themselves in the make-out world imitated the only models which seemed to apply, the men they met; and freshly divorced from adolescence, bedded down freely with them till age twenty-two, three, four, five; and then suddenly a new romantic adolescence seemed to suffuse their plaintive, cock-thrust souls. Dreams. Love. They wanted soul-touching, not just fun-and-fuck. They wanted to think of love and babies and forevermore nearly true: mortality overtook them, and they considered not further defiance but accommodation; and oddly enough, in this accommodation, they needed a place for faith, ring, ceremony, hand-in-hand trueness. Those lines around the eyes meant the beginning of sexual depth. The pools of melancholy beneath the eyes meant the beginning of sexual depth. The recollection of disappointment without the sourness of deception meant that this was a woman, truly; it happened to some of them, and even LaRue and I, sometimes writers-in-residence, were not unmoved.

But while the women began to grow up, we had distractions to help us remain children—money, renown, entertainment, ambition, tireless vanity. Funny Terry Southern played these games at a high pitch, cutting the ground from beneath his own feet. At George Plimpton's house he spilled a drink on Ann Kazin's dress and then bawled, "Oh man, I'm sorry, now your husband won't review my book." He was broken-hearted and tickled.

In another corner Norman Mailer played the eye-fighting game, staring down his opponent, one of the competition, until the opponent pursed his lips and kissed the air at him.

"Um, these are America's great writers?" asked a visiting Italian publisher.

The artists flooded into the waiting rooms of critics, promoters, patrons, grant-givers, and all sent through the same message:

Man here. Says he's different.

And the word came back: "Show me. Throw a typewriter through the window, lecture a President, do a dirty thing on the Susskind show."

Frozen novelists, searching acclaim without doing the work, made a glory of their own impotence and prescribed a remedy of orgies, complained of voyeurism and had themselves secretly filmed "doing it," in full wail diagnosed a universe filled with cancer, giving them cancer, but suffered, in fact, from hemorrhoids. Obstreperous careerists said they were shouting because the world was deaf to them, but the truth was that they couldn't hear their own voices. Confession became a means to celebrity in a time when weakness was the shrewdest means to power, provided it was arrogant enough. Openly they practiced fancy prose. Secretly they sought soft stools.

I thought to leave Manhattan, I knew it was time, when an acquaintance with whom I had shared a cab once to the Village, and with whom I had also stood around at dozens of parties, passed on some silly gossip about me.

When I confronted him, he said bravely, "Yes, I said it. Well, that's my opinion."

"But do you know me?"

"Yes."

"Have we ever talked? Have we ever been out of a crowd together? Have we ever done more than share a cab?"

He looked pensive. "You're right," he said. "But I thought I knew you."

The worst of it was that with marvelous Manhattan snap judgment, I thought I knew him, too.

The New York Breakdown comes from scratching the Manhattan Itch. The good student of New York is successful, and success brings the trouble. The standards, claims, and opinions of others—"That's what they're doing"—fit the requirements of the market. And then what?

I had no job, no need to work. I was free to sleep all day, just so long as I found the nervous energy to embrace the typewriter for an hour or two and let it rattle. I was indulged by agents, publishers, editors. I didn't eat my breakfast standing up at Nedick's; I emerged blinking into the yellowish midmorning light to take eggs at ten forty-five, just before the eleven o'clock Special went off. I was fenced away from the working world. I hardly saw anyone out of the literary life except my Greenwich Village doctor who treated me for persistent colds—and he had been recommended by two novelists, a ghostwriter for a columnist, and the editor of *Nugget*. I yearned to speak with real people so much that I bought shirts I didn't need: Shirt-Buying Adventure; or browsed in museums—Museum Adventure; or went to bed with girls I didn't like—Fuck Adventure.

The ancient dream of community was submerged for many, for me too, in a modern fantasy of celebrity—fame, riches, and the love of women desired by others. Bohemia was coming into vogue, setting styles. Monday evenings at George Plimpton's really were fun, weren't they? And the fashion editors were paying attention, along with the fashionable editors. The West Fourth Street Espresso Cowboys were riding the rails up to Radio Liberation on Times Square to discuss the anniversary of Chekov or "The Influence of Polish Writers Such as Joseph Conrad on Me." It was taped to inspire the crouching, heroic, radio-listening peasants Behind the Iron Curtain. It was only fifty dollars, but afterwards there might be lunch with Santha Rama Rau, and anyway, a fellow can always use fifty dollars, can't you?

Limit purposes.

Circumscribe ambitions.

Get a little cash and save an evening from boredom.

Limit talent, limit risks, and limit losses.

The normal madness of business was imported into the unusual madness of writers making out. Beatness was salable. *Paris Review*ness was salable. "Young novelists" were in demand as the air smogged over in the late fifties. (Sometimes they had crew-cuts, neatly trimmed mustaches, and faithful wives who waited in Westport for them to return from three-day raids in Manhattan, which they invaded with pockets full of hard-boiled eggs against hunger and bennies to keep them up as they met the people who really counted.) Girls, money, and fame were attached to bodies like false limbs. Unleash the straps for love, age, family, death, or even a mere time of retreat and privacy, and it turns out that the Bearer has made himself into an abstract idea, not a man.

Why be so hard on lonely New York?

If there were a God, He would be lonely, too.

The party lasts till dawn. I walk home, jittering high and low, and read *The New York Times* (John Foster Dulles says something, Ike says he's right). As the yolky sun streams through my window, I feel wide awake and famished and go back downstairs, shady-eyed, for early eggs. "Hi there," says Jimmy, "you up betimes? or a late mission, hm?"

"You're right, John," I say, and he says reproachfully, *It's Jimmy.*

Then, dead on my feet despite the coffee, I finally stagger up to bed. It's nine o'clock. Thin dreams of wandering. I hear the mail slid under the door. I take two bites from an apple, think of getting the mail, fall back asleep.

Dream of hallways. Riveting sounds. Endless locked doors.

When I awake, in late afternoon, it's getting dark. No point in working today. No chance to work. Time for another party, another night. The day and life are turned around. Night and party—looking for what? looking for whom?— have replaced it. Nervous time in the city.

Maybe the magik lady that night. LaRue gave me a rubber stamp for my birthday:

Magik Lady Come Soon Now

"Use it and good luck," he said.

"Probably it'll work better'n what I've been using," I said, "and thanks."

Taxi uptown or downtown, into gallery for opening or up to loft for farewell to abstract expressionist on a Prix de Rome. I hide my madness from everyone, but my friend George Elliott says to me, "You're a little insane at parties, just at parties"—and we plan to go for a walk on Riverside Drive tomorrow, when I'll probably not be insane.

There is a girl I like, we trust each other, an arrangement

for joint pleasures, enterprises, expeditions, entertainments. She is a sweet person who deserves better of me, of herself; yet she, too, settles for a comfortable arrangement. We never quarrel. I just go away to Detroit to visit my daughters, write her a note goodbye, and that's that.

Alone again for partying and hunting the magik lady. I doubted she would kiss me into a prince. I began to think I was a closet neuter. I slept till dark, day after day, the soot of New York clogging my nostrils when I awoke. I cleaned myself up, made coffee, returned into the writing factory six feet away from my bed. Dark on a winter day, dark on a spring day. And then out onto West Eighth Street, smiling, because smiling is the way to get along with anyone not of your own family. I had no family here. I was working in this town. Success is the only success Manhattan knows. "Reuben Flair" got checks from magazines, and so did Herbert Gold. Horrid who-am-I questions.

Naturally there was relief and pleasure. Otherwise I wouldn't have been able to tell myself what a good time I was having. Sometimes Saul Bellow came down from his country house on the Hudson River to stay with me. I babbled all morning, telling him what I thought about life, or thought I thought, and listening to the verdict; he lay some of his own troubles in perspective against the plight of the universe; and then we returned to the factory and I went to sleep on the couch while he wrote.

When I awakened, I saw him leaning back in his chair and examining me with those dark, pleading, boyish eyes. "You're okay if you can sleep," he said. "Float down the river, that's right. I admire that."

It was a compliment to be treasured as I always perversely most treasure the unmerited ones. I could sleep, but nerves showed me limits in other ways. I could write, but I began to see through the paper to the rubber roller beneath. I was writing on my own body, it seemed. The palimpsest was being written over.

And then I couldn't sleep, either.

I was alone at dawn. When I awoke, I couldn't remember what I'd done the night before. The door to the medicine chest fell open. A tube, a toothbrush toppled. Sickness in the middle of the night as I searched a remedy. I dreamt of round water in a rectangular basin. It wasn't ice. It was just round water. The basin was long, with curving corners, but definitely rectangular. The water was round.

I was sleeping again, dreaming of distortion. Warp was life. The uncanny truth of Manhattan was that nightmare seemed more stenchy and real than my somnambulating reality, for when I looked again at the nightmare, I was awake and moving in it, like the voodooists possessed by the ancient gods of Haiti. In the evening, awake and moving, I merely smiled as if I ran things, like a voodoo priest or a headwaiter.

What kept me alive was that I kept leaving New York on various travels—to universities, to Cuba, to Europe, to Yaddo, to the midwest to see my daughters and parents—and during these spaces of absence from the boiling city, I did the writing from that time which I still value. On trains and ships, in motels and under the sun on tropical rooftops, I invented moments of calm and quest, suffered the blessed exhilaration of heart pounding, head congested, pen wriggling, typewriter leaping. I felt I was telling my truth during a three-day storm in a battered cheap hotel in Key West with palm fronds slapping against my window. I was even able to write a story, "What's Become of Your Creature?," in my childhood room, in my parents' house in Cleveland, at my maple desk from the Furn Mart, and this was a new stage in my life: able to do it in my parents' house, despite my mother's asking why I was so thin and did I remember Stanley Strassberg, he survived a kamikaze attack but then got his brains washed from drinking too much coffee.

"Mother, I'm working."

"You're writing. He was a captain, it did things to him Mrs. Strassberg won't even tell me about, maybe she doesn't even know, he was perfectly fine, but then he got a coffee habit when he got home—"

"Later, I'm busy, Mother."

"You're writing. Five cups in the morning, he must have been peeing Maxwell House, then he started on the afternoon, that's all he did, naturally he cracked up a regular nervous breakdown—"

"Mother, please."

"Why don't I take away this tray with this phooey stuff and I'll bring you a nice cold glass of guaranteed low-fat?"

But I finished the story. It was more than I could do in Manhattan. In the factory I continued projects, made money, revised manuscripts, discussed assignments, organized notes and fabricated outlines, but I didn't do any real writing in New York. I thought I did, but as I recall those years, everything began and grew in the elsewheres to which I fled on one excuse or another. Elsewheres from which I longed to return to the anonymous pledges of the city.

Often the mail brought temptations to hurry back. Once a telephone call to Saratoga Springs puzzled me with a raveled mystery. "Let me not try to explain this fully except in person," stated the young man whom I'll call Bruce Zebra. "I have a concept here, Herb. I want you to meet us and get a good feel of our plan and organization. We've investigated you thoroughly—in fact, read everything you've written, Herb. I may call you Herb? I know you so thoroughly?—and it's only fair that you proceed with equal caution and go at us top to toe." This was a daring invitation. I wondered what Bruce looked like. "But hurry, Herb, this is not a matter we can let pend indefinitely."

And so, without hurry, with due caution, but of course with pell-mell and non-pending curiosity, I returned to New York to meet the young man, who, while I ignorantly slept, had convened with his friends and colleagues to decide that their mission in life was to make me rich and famous, available to the love of beautiful women and the determined attention of celebrity, without any cost or other obligation to me. Hi there, Dr. Brucie Faustus.

They quartered in space decorated as the main office of a children's products design company. Uncle Wigglys and Mr. Pigglys and funny little squigglies covered the walls, which were all done in primary colors. The yellow and red working desks looked out onto scenes of little orphan whozits painted on Prince Valiant backdrops. The shower of merrie Muzak from the ceiling had been turned off; black holes where franchise operators had confiscated the Bing Crosby and Danny Kaye squads. Rails along the walls and pint-sized furniture proved that at some time in the past, little ones were brought onto the spot to test-market the product. I thought I saw a few throw-up smudges, well-Clorox'd, on the mural of King Arthur presenting Excalibur to Shirley Temple while Jack applauded from a good seat on top of his beanstalk and Jill fetched a pail of Kool-aid.

Zebra Associates were not dealing in children, however. They leased the space from a bankruptcy referee who had taken over for the defunct kiddie operation which had spent all its resources on office decoration. "Madness," said Bruce Zebra, "delusions of grandeur, y'know, Herb? Craziness pure and simplistic. Well, we're the ones to benefit, are we not?"

He stood up from a giant-sized old-fashioned children's

school desk with an inkwell which was perfectly proportioned but large enough to fit a malted milk container. There were purling shreds of wax where, indeed, malted milks to go had rested in the inkwell hole. He was pumping my hand with the power of a former crewman, fortified by malt. It was beyond belief to meet me at last, he declared. When I agreed to consider his proposal, he, together with his associates, had celebrated by taking the rest of the afternoon off. Then they worked on the whole evening through. They had this neat portfolio of plans. If their test-marketing worked, they might go on to other products, but they could guarantee me an exclusivity in my field. It was not clear yet?

"To business," Bruce said. And then faced down my last possible doubts with manly frankness: "I look young?" he asked. "Shit, I'll give you my vitae. I *am* young," he said, "twenty-eight, not to cut any corners on it. Princeton. Wharton Business. Dad was president of . . ." He named a failed automobile company. "I was always raised for heavy industry, but my own natural bent and yearning is toward consumer product such as literature. You've heard of the Oedipus Complex, I'm sure, Herb, though I notice you never mention it in your writings? your works?"

"Well, I'm not sure, Bruce."

"Well, it's not a fatal lack, Herb. One thing I'll not do, not ever in my life, as long as we're associated, and that's tell you how to write. You do your thing and I'll do mine and that way we'll get along just fine."

Fair, blue-eyed, plumpish, shortish, wide-rumped Bruce looked like a man who would get along just fine. His father had been president of a large, albeit extinct company, but he was modest about his oedipal claims. He was bright and assertive, and wished everyone well, especially me. A flat lock of flaxen hair fell boyishly across his forehead as he explained his plan.

"Okay, so we're in PR. But we have this idea that writers are getting to be stars, really make it. But if you're gonna make it, you got to treat it like anyone else who makes it. With P.R. Hell, even Charlie de Gaulle has what's-his-name, Malraux—"

"He had a war going for him, too."

Reproachfully Bruce's bright blue eyes closed in on my crocodile ones. "I didn't say you could do it without talent to begin with. You got to have the raw material, the product. Malraux had that, sure. The underground and Joan of Arc and all that blah-blah-blah, y'understand?"

"Sure, I'm sorry."

"No harm done, Herb. Okay, how much you make a year?"

I named the modest figure. I survived. I supported my children. Bruce whistled. "That's a shame," he said, "a dirty rotten shame. I knew it was bad, but that bad I didn't know. Okay, here's the setup: You don't pay us anything. We work for you free. With taste, fella, subtly, nothing to ruin a very clean image. And then anything over a hundred thousand a year, you split it with us."

It was my turn to whistle, though I didn't. "How on earth do you expect me to be getting a hundred thousand a year?"

"That's only the start. We don't get ours till you get *over*. Naturally it means a movie sale or two, the biggies like that. We think we can help, it's a calculated risk—the column items, the talk shows, getting you before the public. Oh, we work on the people. Reporters. You'll develop a character, Herb."

I begin to fog over in the head. "Why me, Bruce, why me?"

He sent away his secretary, who had appeared in response to his whistle of a few seconds back. She wanted to know what flavor of malted I preferred. He explained that he was only whistling out of shock at something I had said. But maybe I really wanted a malted? He found that one picked him up, two made him sleepy. Maybe I'd like one? Linda waited. No? Linda departed.

Okay, to answer my question, which was why me, Bruce, to share fifty-fifty on everything per year over a hundred thou, he would now proceed to tell me the crucial deal on myself. He counted off my virtues on his fingers. "You're prolific, you're healthy, you're well-begun." This left several fingers for chance discoveries. "Actuarily, you're ahead. We don't require a physical, of course. People we respect respect you. Shit, that's enough for me. I have respect for people I trust, Herb. You meet our guesstimate on the market. Of course, who can tell? All doctors used to drive the Packard, and now look. But my associates and I do the best we can." He noticed the extra fingers and began counting again. "You're Jewish, too, and we don't underestimate it. It's the coming thing. That's part of our total overview."

"You're not."

"No, but, well, I value it, Herb. I'm learning. I'm not such an anti-Semite any more. I've wiped Grosse Point out of my past, Herb. Hell, one of my associates is a Jewish boy and we get along just super. In fact, he's essential in your case, we couldn't do you without Larry Fine." Modestly he lowered his fine blue eyes under the fine blond lashes. "You'll meet him right quick now."

Can I say I was absolutely not tempted? No, I let the dream roll over me. Money and fame equal glory. And glory means I have made something beautiful. And isn't that what I was trying to do? Well, I left some gaps in the logic; passion leaves gaps. This was the time when Jack Kerouac, all aflame, had rushed into town, packaging and selling himself, a meteor describing his own trajectory, and three dozen young English instructors were doing their best by writing their articles for *PMLA* or *College English* or *The Nation* on "Oral Language in Kerouac," "Beat Method vs. Beat Mystique," "Sources of the Kerouackian Novel: Picar as Hitchhiker." And I had gone to college with the founder of oral language. Just because he was better at packaging, why should I fall behind? It would also be a blessing to the tenure-seekers to find a new subject for their bibliographies.

Passion leaves gaps in both logic and feeling. Other writers speeded down from Westport on wings of Dexedrine to do this job. Some stayed in the Village or Brooklyn Heights and had a talent for it. "If we can do you good, Herb, I'll be a contented P.R. executive." Bruce was leading me past the gaily painted children's desks, stuffed toys, and alphabet-lettered office equipment into inner cubicles, a Dutch playhouse, an old-woman's shoe, a cunning troll-bridge, where his associates dwelled. They had their pegboards cleared. They were waiting. I met them one by one. Businesslike Hank with his pipe in his mouth; Linda, our all-around girl, types, shorthands, gets a fantastic rare hamburger and fruit salad from the take-out downstairs; Carl—oh-oh, I guess he's in the peepeetorium, we'll catch him later; and now Larry, the Biggie in your case, Herb.

Larry was my writer. You see, counting on these massive infusions of movie sales, reprinters, musicals, book clubs, suchlike, you need to generate a case of household wordness for the product, you get a barrage going, the items to Leonard Lyons, the calls to that cute little red-haired twitch who works for David Susskind, the Earl Wilson interview—well, you can't be bothered personally with those things, Herb. You're too busy creating the basic product. So it's Larry Fine here, getting to know you, speaking your heart with his typewriter, who sends out the poop. An example? Oh, you know. Dot dot dot Novelist Herb Gold, whose new book *The Optimist* deals with—well, strike that. Start slow and easy. Dot dot dot Novelist Herb Gold says the trouble with American women is, and then it's blah-blah-blah, thanks to Larry Fine — Larry Fine the Writer was smiling and nodding at me, Larry Fine the Herbert Gold Surrogate was winking and sucking on his pipe, Larry Fine would listen to Bruce and then find out all about me so he could speak my truest thoughts for me while I was busy with essential matters, the immortal truth & beauty product. "And then we phone it in to Leonard. Okay, after a couple items, he wants to meet you at the Four Seasons. Okay, we arrange that, too."

"Does Larry eat lunch for me?"

Bruce opened his mouth in the silent-laughter demonstration. "Aw, come on, Herb. Larry knows you're a kidder, too, and that's a thing we all enjoy about you, huh, Larry?" Larry noted it through a blocked strand of clicking wet tobacco. Bruce winked. "You know how it is with us goyish corporations. The one Jew, he's in research & development. Well, that's Larry. We're too small to have a controller, you know, the finance man, like Dad did, but you know what I mean, Herb. Shit, Larry's one heck of a guy. He's a real treat. You two just talk to each other and he'll analyze you through and through. A thing I'd hate myself forever is he made you say something you wouldn't want to say. You wouldn't ever do that, would you, Larry?"

Larry gurgled on his pipe. Oddly enough, I can't recall Herbert Gold's writer ever uttering a word with, you know, syllables, consonants, vowels, accent, maybe a little caesura, all that normal pronouncing language stuff. He may have been cautious, listening, or saving his verbal strength for the cause. He was one of the last of the old-time great pipe-smokers.

Bruce was drawing the mental picture for me. They would do the work, the pleasure would be all mine. Larry would take care of the semantics and I could relax and enjoy myself. And just speaking of those couple lunches at the Four Seasons, he could tell already I'd handle myself like a man. "You'll like Leonard, he'll like you. Listen, Leonard's got to be tired of Truman Capote, Gore Vidal, Norman Mailer, Speed Lamkin, Farley Granger, Arthur Schlesinger Junior— flashes in the pan. He needs new blood, too. And I think Leonard'll genuinely like you, Herb, I really mean that. Larry'll give you lots of items for Leonard. A lunch every few months, what does it hurt you?"

My liver. My heart. My glory.

Their package. Their product.

My sanity.

I told that nice Bruce Zebra in his brightly decorated bankrupt children's product design company that I would not stop thinking about his proposal until it was all clear in my head. He went on explaining about the escalation effect, how movie producers panic when they think there is bidding, about building excitement and a name, about the loneliness of buyers who want to buy an approved product, about how you make one good deal and they all click into place, about how paperback and book club and film and stage and musical and TV and foreign and Pulitzer and Nobel, not to speak of Braille and sweatshirt rights, knickknacks for the knickknack shelf, all seem to come in clusters when people start whispering, about subliminal and liminal, about religion and science, about Dichter and Freud and Bruce's own thesis on marketing non-commodity items at Wharton . . . I believe he recognized that I was promising to consider the campaign (he even mentioned Spanish serialization in *La Prensa,* leaving no corner unturned), but in fact I had finished about it; and even Associate Larry Fine, with his polite death-rattle gurgles, when he closed his cubicle door and continued making notes onto his legal-size pad, knew this brief exploratory meeting would be our last one.

Did I give Bruce Zebra and his plans for me another turn around the head after I descended into the bracing acid air of Madison Avenue? (There was that rare yellowish midtown sun, and a fleet energy in the lungs, and my legs took me all the way down to the Village, feeling good, like an escaped con who has found a stash of clothes and money.) No, not much thought for Zebra Associates. Not even moral disapproval. Only that it was not for me. For someone else, maybe, but not me. And then it would be funny when it would be for someone else. Funny for Zebra, funny for the writer, funny for Manhattan and the whole publishing, perishing world. But I knew all that action would tucker me out. Surely by my life I had put myself in the way of Zebra's invitation. So much complicity in it I must surely admit. But I wanted fame, riches, and the love of beautiful women as reward only for the greatest pleasure of them all, my magic dreams, and the interference of Zebra made me feel as if I were locked into someone else's dream. So much complicity I still denied.

"We want to hear from you real soon!" Bruce cried at the elevator as he saw me out. "It costs you not penny one!" He held the door a moment with a brawny arm, and beneath the gray flannel suit of the time, I suddenly imagined the tanned Grosse Point flesh with downy blond hair all over his body. Yet he had this yearning soul, just like mine. The elevator door was jerking and making little hiccuping noises. Bruce finished first. "We're waiting amidst our toys, Herb," he said, "surrounded by our toys from the toy company which they left behind, but you're the one we really want to play with, Herb."

Nineteen sixty, coming soon, would be one of those rare markers which really sign on a new generation, a set of revolutions. The children of World War II were as far from Hitler as I was from the Kaiser. This had been that ancient decade when Bobby Dylan was still a boy, fresh-come to the great city, and with a girl on Bleecker Street I heard the suicide wail of the kid in some coffee house where they passed the hat. "Pledging the time to you," he sang; and we smiled because this new thing was so peculiarly babyish, whining, and yet winning: beatniks, we thought. They had more life in them than you'd ever suspect from seeing crazy Kerouac reel across a stage, tears in his eyes because he was so misunderstood. "I'm pledging my time to you, hoping you'll come through," I think Dylan sang.

Evenings on the East Side with the record player piled with Frank Sinatra ballads were not what my evenings were supposed to be about as the decade ended. Rastignac and Dick Whittington came to the City for other reasons, to cast out a challenge to more than girls and money. The Eisenhower doldrums didn't excuse our troubles. Will success spoil Vikki Duggan? Is she a great star now—like Jean Shrimpton? The loneliness of girls just trying to make out and please, too many pretty girls, too many clever ones, too many girls trying, their hollow eyes in hollow-pool faces—that didn't excuse us, either. A chic young woman watched my face as she rose like the moon over me, asking *Do you like this? Do you like this? Is this what you like?* I've already mentioned the pillow thrown into the alley, soaked with another girl's tears

—oh, no proper war against her. This was not the place to fight the war.

In the community of girls and the commerce of culture, I forgot I was a writer, a Jew, a man. I was a clever merchant who did his best to present body and soul to an audience of beds and contracts. Those poor girls, sad friends, distracted consumers, and that forlorn, light-spirited self. Like the Hasidic folk singer, I was elsewhere than at home in the Diaspora.

My elder daughter drew flowers with laundry markers on shirt cardboard, wrote Flowers for My Daddy, dated it, put her age on it—ten years old. I dreamily indulged in writing (my own), harshly chopped at the typewriter (my factory for other purposes), and was weary of the division of labor into money and soul. I liked eating Italian ices with Mary Emma Elliott. I liked options for movies and plays, those expense-account lunches at Sardi's. I liked adventuring in the evening. I liked talking it over with LaRue. I hated my life.

The leaders of this youth society, just then discovering the Discotheque, one of the Great Ideas of the Western World in the late fifties, were older than F. Scott Fitzgerald when he cracked up. *Moby Dick* was finished when Melville was thirty-four, Jesus died for the sins of others at thirty-three, Young Writers were pushing forty and collecting grants. The kid Bobby Dylan was beginning to sing in coffee houses on Bleecker and MacDougal streets about how he finally got a job in New York town. He sounded like a hillbilly and they wanted folk singers, but they paid him a dollar a day anyway. Howdy, New York.

Citybilly creep. Handfuls of gritty rain. Insidious with recollections and nostalgia, I was joining the peculiar company of those who seize avidly upon each moment as if it and only it means life. And it meant nothing. And we seized upon projects and plans, advances, options, schedules for the future, as if they, too, meant life. And they meant nothing, either. No meaning, no community, and the moments and the plans are not enough despite the jerk of excitement. A contract or a conquest, a few good words one morning or a telephone call from an agent in the afternoon, and the voice in the factory told itself (the voice talking to itself because all those who might understand it were busy running their own factories): "I've done it! I've really done it this time! I've made it!"

They sure had a lot of gall. I had a lot of gall. That's how it was.

THREE

12

What was I doing in Europe again? Nothing very much. Getting away. Sitting in cafés in that familiar clamor of Paris to write in a notebook, the straw wiggling between my fingers, prying into the past and fantasy for some sense for today and reality. I thought I could tickle open the closed doors. This is the persistent dream of the writer, no matter how many times he opens the door for a moment and then sees it swing impenetrably once more shut.

Like love, the straw between the fingers gives moments of ecstasy and no final act of discovery. Like love, it promises to make sense of meaning and meaninglessness, and gives mere joy. It celebrates for a moment. It changes not so much as it thinks to change.

Well then, why not try getting further away?

Flight is never merely away from something. It intends to go toward something, too, even if it knows not what.

During this late spring of 1958 a sleepy general reigned in Washington; an alert one was just coming to reign in Paris amid the flowering plane trees and the last explosions of the *plastiques*. I had obliging company for the evenings, rue St.-Severin, Place St.-André-des-Arts, but I moved on. I took a train from Paris to Marseilles and closed my eyes in the *couchette* out of the Gare de Lyon. No sense looking for another nice French girl, the gray-flecked dandy's familiar salvation; that road back from melancholia has been followed so often it's littered with dried flowers, tangled sheets, crooked smiles, temporary promises. A Danish or a Swedish adventure on the express from Paris to Marseilles is the same with fresher smells, another victory over objects; there's a limit to the collection of such victories. A meridional lady from the streets of Marseilles with plump thighs and dark eyes? No, no, a mere change of brand and label. There must be another way.

I was melancholic and unwilling to be pleasured any longer in tourist fashion—girls, food and wine, architecture, museums, music, churches. The theater made me sleepy and they talked too fast. I liked drinking my coffee afterwards amid the crowd at the café on the corner, but the parade had gone around the boulevard and the same players were coming back for another cameo appearance. My notebook, which had given me so much joy, began to seem like the drunkard's bottle. Into it I sucked cleverness, regret, resolutions, a stench of fantasy, and tomorrow began the same old tricks. One night I forgot it at a Café Sportif, or maybe it was at the Café du Port, began to shake with anxiety when I noticed it was gone, and therefore, a repenting wordaholic, resolved to do without it. Perhaps the black-aproned Madame Patronne still keeps it under the counter near her stool with the cigarets, matches, and Olympia Press Books.

Surely I must be growing old, all but my legs, which walked me tirelessly about the southern city. One afternoon I hiked out to Le Corbusier's Cité Lumière, and saw how it had grown shabby, veined with hairline cracks in the cement, but there was a noisy market on the fourth floor, a smell of leafy vegetables, sand and wet, a medieval market-place accumulation, and a café on the roof of the classic skyscraper machine for living. There was also a playground for children, with concrete free forms to break the kiddies' heads on. I didn't want my children to live away from me in Detroit, but I didn't want them to live in a machine for living, either. I began explaining my theories about architecture to a visiting student from Grenoble.

"Mais pour un américain," she said, *"vous parlez si bien."*

I broke off our discussion. Terrible headache, important telegram, the tour waiting; no, I'm not a writer, but a shoe wholesaler . . . I intended not to climb onto this treadmill once more. It seemed that my Francomania, which I suffered for good but not adequate reasons, a dream of light, ease, history, and style—an indulgence shared with my Haitian friends in Port-au-Prince, who also liked French girls—was fading under the isolation of a long season in France. Surely the bread, wine, language, avenues, gardens, mists, and skies, the proud and prickly erotic gaming, the angry habitual wit of Frenchmen, made a reassuring contact with some part of the past for this *licencié en philo* at the Sorbonne. Some Haitians remembered the Quartier Latin or Montparnasse, the Café de Tournon and bicycling in the Faubourg St.-Germain, and thought they were black Frenchmen. They had left girls in Paris, too, but they weren't black Frenchmen. They weren't, they were strangers in France and in Haiti; and I was no Frenchman, either, even if I had sung with the medical students at the Bal des Quatz Arts, figured out the jokes in the *Canard Enchainé* and read the last articles by Camus in *Combat,* and now returned as a for-mer husband to see a part of my past which I remembered as a long Bastille Day dance, with *bal musette* accordions and colored lights strung across the squares and obliging ladies flashing their eyes at me and . . .

No. There was the Arab who shrieked when we caught him passing counterfeit money in exchange for my GI clothes. There were the nesting would-bees of St.-Germain-des-Prés, now mostly in teaching, advertising, or their fathers' businesses. There was the man with acromegaly, made monstrous by a Nazi doctor's gaming with the pituitary gland, and Schwartz, who wrote a history of the Jewish artists killed by the Germans and dedicated it to the gypsies—both dead now.

No. I wouldn't find myself and wife, the crazy kids in Paris. Find something else then.

Without having thought about it in advance, I wished to see my friend Shimon Tal, the Israeli fishing expert assigned to Haiti by the UN, and I guessed I might just look up some shipping companies in the Marseilles telephone directory and see if there was a way to get to Haifa by boat. No hurry. No appointments anyplace. Why not sail the Mediterranean awhile?

I found a Greek liner called the *Messapia*—Genoa, Naples, Piraeus, Cyprus, and Haifa, making these short stops along the way—and for about eighty dollars they would take me. Why in heaven, asked the shipping agent, would an American choose to travel on such a vessel? The food, he said, *les repas, la foule.* I shrugged. He took account of it and answered with his own shrug. We were communicating in Marseilles. *"Alors bon,"* he said to the row of rubber stamps on his desk as he began tattooing my papers. *"Bon, bon, très bien, bon"*—each nasal punctuating a swing of stamp onto pad, stamp onto document. He had mighty shoulders.

At the dock I watched mourning widows with ant-trails of children board the ship, peasant traders with straw bags and chickens, an Italian band with their greenish instruments, midget Greek sailors hurrying back and forth with bags of potatoes, noodles, and onions for our dining pleasure. No one was polishing brass or scrubbing the decks. The smell of sea was losing against sour civilized smells. The agent at the shipping company must have had something in mind with his celestial question and shrug. Why this ship? Why me? The band set itself up on deck to serenade the travelers and the flapping, cawing gulls. They were playing "Volare." The lyrics sounded like "Eh tutti eh tutti eh tutti," but I was in linguistic lapse. *Volare, cantare;* to fly and to sing, I understood that well enough.

And a girl was standing alone on the desk with a striped duffel bag at her feet. She leaned on the rail and gazed back at the port of Marseilles. There was a tiny chin, and a ripple of water-reflected sunlight on the thin face, and long straight fine hair. She was wearing a belted coat and a peaked student cap under which the hair swirled. And all my resolutions about finding no distractions except the Mediterranean Sea, the crowd of travelers, and my morose stocktaking disappeared. I was interested in but one person in the crowd, that girl, whom I took for a Dane or a Swede.

The Mediterranean lay still under merely decorative little white foamings, unlike the heaving North Atlantic which I had crossed by English liner, and the sun sparkled down through unresisting invisible conduits, setting miniature blazes of reflection on water, wood, and metal. There was a smell of foot-trodden wood rising from the desk, not unpleasant at all, and I felt a lazy anticipation about the girl. I had no doubts about her. I had only enough doubts to give me a dandyish excitement. In the dandy's way, I was willing to give up my melancholia at the prospect of sport. I squinted at sparkles and squiggles in the air, stretched in the warmth, imagined insects decked out in intern's jackets, chasing about in air-motes, and just let my idiot self-amused fancy cook in the sun. The clouds made a dim-brained sky, diluted cranial knoblets floating apart to let the sun through. Instinct instructed me as the sun emerged triumphant and to stay. It was a thin, girlish face and slim body in the tightly belted coat, but there were lines at the mouth and the corners of the eyes and she was not as young as she looked. I would have her.

Now the stevedoring seamen were bringing up halves of lamb, covered with flies. Good, we wouldn't eat just onions and potatoes, though if they didn't get them out of the sun, those split pink lambs, we would have weevils and worms with our *mouton aux mouches.* I would get acquainted soon, but no hurry.

Barrels of wine, too. I took the chance of competition from some Neapolitan trader or Greek widower, but I thought just to establish my lonely presence, plant it in her mind, and then trust to good fortune to keep her cool until after I had a wash and a change of clothes. Portside loading is a sweaty, dusty business in Marseilles. I had never fallen in love with a small-chinned girl before, and this historical observation, trivial as it may seem, blocked out the creak and howl of loading machinery, the din of port machinery, the oom-pah-pah version of "Volare," the smiling, gravy-jowled purser and the sternly senile captain of the *Messapia* with his face like a Montenegrin hero, in later life, on a postage stamp. My senses were mobilized for the game, and in throbbing doubt and cunning, they blocked out the knowledge that this game was not at all about love, despite my old habit of giving it a grand name. Small chin was all I had on my mind—not my distracted soul, distance from my daughters in Detroit, flight from Manhattan, the book I was writing. Small chin and tight-belted coat shouldn't be enough to take me from the prime matters, but they were.

Also slim grace, serious scowl, crooked lean on the railing of the ship. Stupid man I am, I thought; and then, as usual: okay, be stupid, live up fully to the possibilities of stupidity. The engines had been rumbling. We were in motion.

I wandered the ship as it steamed out of harbor. It seemed to carry a superfluity of widows with babies, more than required by fate and statistics, until I realized that these weren't widows, they were only in mourning, and they used cousins from Calabria, uncles in America, dear departed grandparents as sufficient excuse to wear their favorite black vestments. Baskets of food accompanied those who signed on without meals. We ate below in the windowless clatter of a mess hall. Moist onions rubbed deafeningly against gravied noodles, lamb bones echoed in great stewpots. I caught the lady's eye across the room— tiny oval face, fine long narrow brown gaze, careless hair. No smile. I took her melancholic expression for erotic pouting. My reasonless despair had given way to reasonless confidence. I was in no hurry.

That night I prowled the deck. I didn't find her. When I went below, thick kitchen smells, harsh laundry smells assaulted me. I took my blankets and crawled into a lifeboat to sleep in this cradle, waves of warm summer salt seadrift consoling me for patience. Cramped dreams of desire, but then a marvelous long awakening before dawn, the stars winking out one by one as we plowed eastward.

Late on the second morning out, I was sitting on the deck with a copy of *Le Monde*, which I had already read twice, including "Necrologie" and the reviews of "Fêtes et Spectacles." The lady came up, stood nearby, and asked, "You are going to Haifa?"

"Yes, hullo, you?"

"Yes."

"You are a Jew?" she asked.

"American," I said, "yes, I'm Jewish. You're Swedish?"

She smiled. "You recognize my accent, do you?"

I wanted to boast of my accurate ear, but held back out of modesty.

"It is not a Swedish accent, it is rather a Hungarian one," she said. "But a Swedish citizen today." And the smile broadened. "You have been watching me? You saw my passport?"

"No."

"Oh. My clothes? My duffel?"

"Something about you. I have these insights."

"Well, you are very clever. This year I am a Swede. But I was born a Hungarian. And now we are friends, yes?"

"Yes, we sure are," I said.

She sat on the deck beside me, her knees in her arms. We watched the sea, sparkles and tiptop foamings. "To review once more," she said, "you are a Jew?"

"I already answered that question. I'm not going to change my mind." My humor was as infallible as my recognition of Swedish accents.

"And an American?"

"Why do you keep asking?"

She shrugged. Swedes are famously quirky. I would calm all doubts in the interest of the higher cause of understanding with this lovely, small-chinned girl with fret at the corners of eyes and mouth. "I am everything you and I have both just agreed upon," I said.

She smiled like a little girl. It was a lovely, delighted smile.

"Very good. Very, very good."

That was an odd bit of reassuring, but at times like these you don't criticize oddness in a lady. Life can teach a man not to question unnecessarily or even necessarily. I would ride with her the way she seemed to need to ride for those first moments of shipboard acquaintance.

"Um," she said, sitting with me on the deck, elbows on knees, chin in hands. "Nice day. My name is Hannah. You didn't ask my name. Hannah. Would you like to make love?"

We went down to her cabin while I pondered the question. I may have answered or she may have assumed an answer. I was walking, wasn't I?

Mumble mumble funny question mumble.

She had a sly, sideways, welcoming smile in the slatted shadow of her first-class cabin. Rubbed mahogany, a table with a curved edge against tilting seas, a closet with mirror; and in the mirror, a girl was pulling her frock over her head. I didn't believe my eyes. I turned from the mirror to the girl. She slipped off her dress. I felt a swimming horror. How had I sinned? Why was I to be punished now with sudden madness after so little warning?

Her body was deformed, carved up, sculpted into a parody of an erotic demon. There were puckered lips, folds, crevices of flesh, scarred blinking receptacles, tightly pursed mouths, folded cicatrices which twisted like snakes when she moved.

The thin and pretty face smiled at me. "It was an experiment they did," she said. "They had doctors, you know, I think? Who did these experiments. Anything a man could think of. You want?"

No.

"You don't want?" she asked. "Some men like."

At the age of twelve she had been shipped with her mother from Budapest to be used as whores by the Germans. They killed her father. A group of scientists, far from home, lonely for their laboratories and experiments, developed the idea of trying out new sexual machines, inventing novel erotic contraptions to service groups of men, avoiding all danger of individual attachments, removing the sexual machine from comparison with wives, mothers, and sweethearts back home, but giving the doctors a chance to play, giving the men a chance to play, with no loss of consoling human warmth and interesting churning and grasping motions. Some of the girls survived the operations. In this case nothing was lost but a Jewish woman.

Her mother died after the second operation, but she lived. At age thirteen the body recovers somehow and makes do with what it is given. Whatever it was intended to be, it accepted the new installation and grew like a dwarfed or stunted tree.

"Can't the doctors . . . ?" I asked.

"Perhaps," she said. "They tell me they can. They were agreeable to try. The Swedish doctors. They took me to Switzerland and there I was examined by a German doctor." Her eyes glowed, but she refused the excitement of reliving her history. She would not make it new for herself by thinking it through again. She repeated only what she must have said many times before. "I am this way now. I do not wish to be cut and sewed to be another way. So—you want?"

Her name was now, she said, Anna Freiberg.

In Genoa I strolled the streets and found silver rings for my daughters. In Naples I wandered a whole afternoon, lurching with sea legs, and climbed back on board despite a temptation to desert ship and disappear into the blue skies, the frantic arcades, African confusion, Italian laughter.

I drank coffee in Athens, *"pente drachma,* please," and

found the Parthenon and other monuments which I recognized from cards at Taft School in Lakewood—why not stay awhile? Boys followed me among the ruins. Pimps followed me everywhere. I bought an ancient Greek coin with, dimly, the image of Queen Elizabeth wearing through. Back on board after the day. There was a war among Turks, Greeks, and Cypriotes and we didn't make the last scheduled stop.

The port of Haifa looked like Port-au-Prince, white, hot, noisy, with lines of stevedores. There were even some African Jews, felasha, a blue-black gleaming under the sun. The *Messapia* rocked at rest in the landside ebb and flow of oil-smirched water. Another port, this one at a peculiar southeastern corner of the Mediterranean Sea.

I hadn't noticed the customs officials' motorboat tie up, but the Israeli officers in their shorts and jackets, shirts with open collars, knobby knees, looked like colonial Englishmen, except for one, a large fattish young man, who waited shyly on deck. Diplomatic privilege. His wife ran to his arms.

"Otto Freiberg, my husband, the consul for Sweden in Haifa, I present Mr. Gold, who sat at table with me."

He bowed. "Thank you for keeping my wife company," he said.

I must have uttered polite sounds. I fled. Later I waited nearby with my bags. They were speaking rapidly in Swedish. After a moment he put his arm about her in a creaky public gesture of tenderness, and she leaned her head briefly against his shoulder before she pulled away. He was pale and heavy, a ski instructor going to bureaucratic fat, flesh overhanging his collar; he was sweating; his pants had fit him better last year. A crowded crotch with the creases stretched horizontal, a soaked English shirt, shoes with a purplish shine on them, a sweater over his arm. I stared at him amid the distractions of coming to port in Israel. The fair flaxen heap

of Swedish husband was a mystery to me. He loved a muti-
lated bride.

In a country of pioneers Americans feel like visitors from
an ancient Gothic land. A parachutist captain with a droop-
ing handlebar mustache and three pips on his collar, his
golden hair like a Cornwall farmer's, his accent cockney, told
me about fruit trees in South Africa; his family had owned a
plantation for three generations; he had been used to apart-
heid, even the beating of workers on his own farm. "Then
why did you leave?" I asked him.

"I'm a Jew. I love my children. I didn't want them to get
used to it, like me."

My friend Tal worked in the Ministry of Agriculture; I slept
in his borrowed room in Tel Aviv and drove with him to
Kibbutz Nir David. Where the road passed near the Jor-
danian border we stopped the car and took rifles out of the
trunk. They seemed to deprive us of speech. We held our
weapons and waited round the curve of the dusty road, and
then relaxed. "You ever use these?" I asked.

"Not so often," he said. "You are bored in our kibbutz, you
may go back to Tel Aviv with me Monday."

After greeting his wife and children, shy after a week
apart, the assistant undersecretary of agriculture attended to
his duty of handing out hard-boiled eggs and tomatoes in the
dining hall. I told him he looked like a flower girl with his
basket of eggshell white and red. "I am not so pretty as
Haitian lady," he said.

We talked about Haitian girls ("Whatever happened to
Felice Goldenberg, and the beautiful wife of Doctor Assad,
and Olga Silvera?"), and I didn't mention Hannah Freiberg.
Here in Israel, amid a history of so much trouble, no need to
pass on this burden. The sin and horror brought by men onto

earth was not to be unraveled. You begin to unravel mysteries when you find a stray thread, not when there is only a tight and seamless darkness.

I stayed at Kibbutz Nir David long enough to shake off the summer-camp feeling, long enough to learn that Abba and Yma are the Hebrew words for Father and Mother and that the children cry Abba! Abba! Yma! Yma! when they greet their parents at the end of the working day. The children's hour was a time for tea and cakes. Some had hot plates in their cabins; Tal had brought a samovar here after his travels. The *chamsin* winds blew ceaselessly, sweeping cavalries of dust down the roads; blood and orange filled the sky; at sunset the children disappeared into the parents' cabins. A close of day folding inward upon family. A few guards strolled near the tractors, hats pulled down against the slanting sun, collars up against the grit heaving through the Jezreal valley.

I joined the Tals and their daughters in their greedy knee-to-knee devouring of the day's news and little berry cakes. The girls tried to talk English, giggled, returned to Hebrew, teased me, told their stories while their mother poured and their father wiped crumbs from their faces. This concentrated intimacy began by embarrassing the intruder. Then I let myself be as greedy as they were. How could I not compare these parents and children with the son and father I had been? Without telephones, vacuum cleaners, newspapers, or the aimless distractions of city life, these parents and children, eye and flesh, steadily knitted themselves together.

The wide world was not far. Elsewhere on the kibbutz there were two mulatto girls, born of some obscure union in Germany. Some of the older people wore tattooed numbers on their wrists. If there was an Anna Freiberg among them, they never spoke of her. But when a delegation of German agricultural experts wanted to visit Nir David, a meeting was called. The agricultural experts were of the wrong age; old enough.

It was decided to treat them like anyone else, with the usual hospitality of food and lodging. They invited the visitors to stay the night there in the Jezreal valley on the Jordan border, but although most of the kibbutzniks spoke German, all conversation would be in English. They would discuss farming and fish-culture problems in English; they would make politeness over meals in English. The one thing they could not yet bear was to speak German with Germans from Germany.

At the end of the long weekend I drove back to Tel Aviv with Tal. Again the curve of road near the border, and the car stopped, and we picked our weapons from the trunk. Tal didn't carry his rifle except on the small stretch of road where it was the rule. Past the danger zone, he pulled over and we carefully lay the weapons back in the trunk. We picked up two hitchhiking soldiers, swarthy North Africans with curly beards and Uzi submachine guns cradled in their arms. They didn't mind carrying their weapons.

An unhealthy tailpipe went *thunk-thunk-thunk* against the bumper. "You like me to fix that?" the soldier asked. "Just give me a piece of wire, I cut something off, I fix that." We decided not to stop.

In Tel Aviv I took Tal to a play, *The Egg*, which I had seen in Paris and could follow despite my lack of Hebrew. It was about a thirty-year-old cocksman, chasing girls in place of anything else in life to chase. He was a nimble-legged clerk, agile and cheap, and it was a French farce with one shrill line of meaning. I laughed again at the plight of the man who kicks radios to kill them, but instead makes them burst into jazz, and then despite himself, he has to go dancing. His mop of red hair flew. The girls clicked on like the radio. It was close enough to home, to my friend LaRue and me. There was just a glimpse of another possibility. It allowed just as much light and judgment as intelligent French boulevard cynicism allows.

We sat up front, admiring the agile youthful pantomime of the Israeli actor Velikansky. His every gesture—the bounciness on balls of feet, the jack-in-box leap from the knees when he stood up, the self-loving constant wiggling of his body—expressed the body pride of a city man who has nothing but body pride to stand between him and the void. It was the quintessential ever-young stud, making out, making do, and odd to find him here tumbling girls in the language of the prophets.

Later Tal and I took our coffee at the Café Cassit, which was the Tel Aviv version of the Flore in Paris, artists and Bohemians and skinny, lynx-eyed ladies heaving manes of hair when they appreciated the joke. Tal was smiling and saying, "That actor you admire, Velikansky." He pointed to a bald man in a corner with some friends. He was red-faced, skeletal, worn-out, with badly chapped lips and a peeling scalp. He sat slumped in his chair. He was about seventy years old. Now, naked of make-up and wig, he was as different from my idea as Hannah Freiberg had been when she removed her clothes. The agile, jitterbugging young Parisian had disappeared into the worn Russian Jew from the Moscow Art Theater. He suffered from allergies, eczema.

"Tell him," Tal said, "shouldn't you tell him you like his performance? I shall introduce you."

He took me by the elbow. Velikansky smiled through yellowish teeth. I recognized his accent in English—the accent of my father.

He understood my timidity before the uncanny, this old man who was and was not the young man I had seen on stage, and then he shrugged his thin shoulders. "I can manage it from eight-thirty till eleven. I'm seventy-two, alas," he said. "But who can't be thirty for a little while?"

I began nodding in agreement.

"And for a long while if he must?" When he smiled, he put on Felicien Marceau's vision once again. The Paris dude appeared in a crazy, lopsided grin, and then vanished within the old actor's indulgence of an admirer.

"I am like Israel," he said, explaining as Israelis explain everything, "I make myself young by an act of will. Of course, I am tired now and the metaphor is imperfect. I can only make myself young for a few hours every night, beginning at eight-thirty. And now, as you see, I am old once more."

"You're a wonderful actor."

He grinned and winked his bald eyelids and did a little jitterbugging tap with his feet. "I am always young to hear that. Thank you very much." The old man fit himself into the young one like Chinese boxes being folded together for the pleasure of a child. "Please come to our theater again, please," he said. "I also play an old man in *Cherry Orchard*. That too is demanding. A seventy-year-old actor must pretend to be an old man, too, as that man is old, not as *he* is old."

Later Tal indulged me as I explained about acting and gesture, about the power of will, about spirit and body; how a way of getting out of a chair makes a man young, a tilt of the chin, tension of back. Tal didn't waste words. He needed to ask no questions nor provide any answers. He knew I was only explaining to myself about Velikansky and Israel.

Jerusalem, during the tenth anniversary festival of 1958, was a week-long Chinese New Year, Bastille Day, Fourth of July celebration of survival and the beginning of life. The ancient people had been reborn a new nation. I drove the long rocky road, past the rusted-out armored cars and trucks which had been left there since 1948, flowers perpetually sprinkled on them by those who remembered the dead. The joke ran: When it gets too rusty, they haul it away and find another wreck for the tourists. No matter. Men had died. A Yemenite girl I met, a silversmith, had driven one of those trucks and lived. Her partner had died. The whitish mountains above seemed to be circling lazily in the sky. That was vertigo from the speed of our car, screeching around curves in the road with a crazed driver trying to pretend this was a straight Polish boulevard. Slow down, Mr. Warsaw. Ah, better. The Judean hills looked empty and pure above the road, humped sheep browsing on the stalled spaceships.

Even walking in Jerusalem, I felt the low, pure, distant mountains, covered with outcroppings, white limestone it seemed under the sun, bluishly shadowed later in the day, circling slowly about me. I strained to see if the black dots were shepherds moving. Dry, dry, dry, dry, dry, dry was the air. My lips were chapped. My eyes were moist. I felt fine. Here in Jerusalem, home at last, I didn't mind having an old man's dry skin. It wasn't that dry. A little olive oil, a little sweat from dancing, too, would fix me up fine.

The words of Zachariah: "And I said, whither doest thou go, and He said unto me: to measure out Jerusalem and see how much its breadth is and how much its length. Open shall Jerusalem remain because of the many men and beasts in the midst thereof."

In olden times houses could not be sold in this town, but only leased until the Second Coming, when they would be returned to their original owners. I wondered if the kids playing touch football in the street owned their footballs. I wondered if the Israeli officers carrying tennis rackets owned the courts on which they played at dawn, before the scorching sun came up, or only leased them while waiting for the Messiah.

I was visiting the lively family of an Israeli writer and performer, Dahn Ben-Amotz, who was married to Ellen St.-Sure of Oakland, California, whom I had known years ago in New York. The Israeli Bohemian and the long-legged California girl now had sabra sons. I partied with my friends and walked the streets alone at dawn, sunlit noon, midnight. The high bright air of Jerusalem deprived me of sleep and of the need for sleep. When my legs ached with walking, I drank coffee in little cafés until my muscles were twitching to walk again amid the softly glowing umber of Jerusalem stone. The hills had been quarried for thousands of years to create this color for a city.

All my life, sleepless wandering in cities has been the way I have discovered myself. Often the discovery was not very important, a mere itch that kept me awake, a whole adolescence of itches in Lakewood, a sealed head filled with curiosities in New York, Paris, Port-au-Prince, and Detroit. But now, measuring out Jerusalem by foot, I began to see what my nervous pacing through the world had meant. That I was looking and had sometimes found something was clear enough. The meaning of what I found, the interruption, and then the ceaseless renewal of search had been a mystery to me despite all my American meditation on self, on quest and need, and the hope in them. Those days and nights in Jerusalem, hot dry mountain days and cold dry mountain nights, gradually brought me to what I was looking for and what I had already found. Not in one moment of discovery, not in a blinding illumination near a holy place, not through some Islamic, Christian, or Jewish revelation on thrice-blessed ruins, but gradually, listening outside shuttered windows, tiring my body with hiking up and down hills, letting the stony echoes of Jerusalem remind me of what I had never seen before, I came to learn certain secrets about the deals I had made with myself. With magic and community absent, religion and family shriveled, one of them disappeared into dimmest nostalgia, I had put the doubt and gaming of love ahead of all other knowledge, ahead of knowledge itself. Here as elsewhere, I sometimes confused euphoria—a condition of not caring what I was doing and with whom—with ecstasy, in which I might know myself, yet not care, yet care without caring. I had dwelled in a confused American effort to make a temple of desire, and worship in it, and to make a resurrection of occasionally gratified desire.

After childhood, men understand that knowing the truth does not always change their lives. And so the truth was still not enough.

In this time of festival in Jerusalem, I also found a French circus and carnival, La Fête Foraine de Toulon, marching with drums, fifes, and one small elephant that I imagined unfolded from a box, wash-and-dry, after the trip from Marseilles. Its trunk had coiled wrinkles on it, like my nylon shirt, imperfectly heat-treated, with a plastic that peeled off the fabric. The elephant walked slowly, swinging its wrinkled trunk and showing brown tusks, as if it had been chewing tobacco, to the street crowd of children, most of them born since Israel became a nation, since that night on the Upper West Side of Manhattan when I danced in the street with a lady and asked her to make me a happy groom . . . My own children were now with their mother, my former wife, in Detroit.

I followed the parade to the circus ground on an outlying terrain of foot-pounded earth. Sawdust smells, cotton candy, and a babble of Mediterranean voices made it seem more

like the Elks Field in Lakewood, Ohio, than the land of my
ancestors, but it was a French circus with Jewish acrobats.
Jewish acrobats. I expected to see Velikansky grinning in
tights and hanging from a trapeze by his teeth, waving hello
with ankles which were not arthritic during working hours.
A tattooed muscle-man, thighs bulging in striped tights,
chest naked and heaving, swung on the balls of his feet
through a crowd which parted like the Red Sea before him.
"Le Superman Tatoúe," a North African boy whispered as he
passed, and the benevolent monster paused, turned, and
flashed him a sawmill face full of teeth, tousled the mass of
mahogany curls, and answered, "Shalom!" The boy shrieked
with joy. His mother clutched him. His father, a man with a
dead eye turned up and bluish, yawned and looked away, as
if dwarfs, kangaroos, cotton candy, anything at all on earth
or in heaven, future or past, imagined or dreaded, was of
more interest to him than this muscled giant. He didn't cover
his mouth. The giant moved toward his tent and the thrilled
boy was explaining, explaining to his father in what sounded
like guttural Arabic—perhaps it was Hebrew—what they
had just seen, what his father had missed, lost in a wilderness
of jealous boredom.

The carousel turned, grinding out the music of carnival.
Harshly amplified voices of pitchmen rose above the noises.
I stood in the crowd and scuffed through the light snowfall
of sawdust to the whitish packed earth beneath, stamped
tight by feet, thousands of years of feet, like the magic paths
behind billboards in the primeval forests of undeveloped lots
in Lakewood, stamped tight, we believed, by Indians,
depression hoboes, and furtive wet-eyed fiends. I had invented a myth for Lakewood when the myths of Jerusalem
lay undiscovered. Now I strolled like a yokel in the place of
my ancestors, gaping at circus workers who looked like gyp-

sies and spoke Yiddish or French, odder than any freaks I had seen in the carnivals of Georgia, the Carolinas, or southern Ohio. They were Polish. They spoke Yiddish. They were Moroccan. They spoke Spanish. They were Tunisian. They spoke Hebrew and French. They were French and blond and spoke Yiddish and had come from Poland or Lithuania or slave labor camps in Germany. Some of them walked horses and zebras and elephants which were leased, not owned, until the Messiah would appear and they might return to their original proprietors.

I wondered if there was a cage with freaks, a prognathic monster like the damaged creature I knew in Paris—oh, his tongue, jaw, and ears had stopped growing, he was dead now. This circus would not display freaks constructed by Nazi doctors. When the man with acromegaly returned to earth, he would be a slim young scholar, the boy from Lodz before the war.

I ate choumous, a spicy grainy mush scooped onto flat bread. I had a sandwich of tomatoes, onion, cucumbers, the vinegar juice running down my cheeks. There were other stains on the Haspel cord summer suit. Someday it would be marvelously dry-cleaned by the Messiah's advent.

The night before the climax of this tenth anniversary festival, a parade through Jerusalem, I went to a party with my friends. All day long there were dancing celebrations like weddings in the hot dry city, and all night long there were parties and singing and dancing, like weddings, in the cool dry city. It seemed there were no outsiders any more. The many accents were all home accents. We danced. Parties everywhere, lights, strings of lights, music, and tireless dancing. We drank. There was a girl I found pretty enough, and after dancing and drinking, I found her beautiful. Her name was Nachamah and I walked her home in the middle of the

night. She led me through the dark, irregularly angled, ancient streets and I wondered how I could find my way back
and I didn't care. "You like Israel?" she asked.

"Yes."

"You like me?"

"Yes."

"You crazy?"

"I think so," I said. I was lost and sane. "No, I feel fine."

"Do I talk too much?"

I thought about saying yes to this, too. But it would break
the mood. "Maybe," I said.

She answered something. I was thinking confused ginny
thoughts about Bastille Day in Paris during my student days.
How different this was. Those who had torn down the Bastille
were still alive, still ardent, still ready for their wars. History
and the celebrators of history were contemporary with each
other.

"Then come upstairs," she had answered.

Near dawn I was heading back through crooked streets
toward the house of my friends. My legs were made of rubber, so I was sure they wouldn't break. They might bend and
wobble, but I would bounce if I fell. I didn't feel tired, I was
exalted, my legs were also made of laughter. Amid the
hushed nighttime loveliness of Jerusalem, I heard strange
sounds and laughter again, the dancing and lovemaking continuing all around me from the reawakened young of this
ancient city. Predawn birds were twittering from roofs.
Sometimes an abrupt breakfasting shadow swept toward the
street and then back up to its perch. Against the night sky I
looked for pale silhouettes of the Judean hills. The shadows
were visible. Those hills have been so printed in our imagina-

tions, and in so many ways, that love of them is almost a reflex, like the love of parents and children.

Awe. Who was I to have sticky legs again?

Dread. Where else might I wander?

Nowhere. Nowhere. Nowhere.

I might live elsewhere than home, but this was home.

And yet what I began to feel, though I would never need sleep again, was mere fatigue. There were cats slinking through the alleys, just like the cats of Paris. This was also a place like other places.

I wandered through Jerusalem like travelers everywhere, breaking out of the box of family by bumping heads through strange doorways. I wanted ease and pleasure, but was seeking something else. I was sick of too much turmoil in my heart, and seeking nothing. How many Jews have dreamed of sending themselves as messengers to God in Zion? I was sending myself as messenger to myself, and what was the message I brought? That I was moved by my kind. A simple message. That the history of the lost Jews of Lakewood and Haiti, and of the Auschwitz survivor Schwartz, who dedicated his book to the murdered gypsies, could all come to this: a man walking across Jerusalem at night after a party and taking a girl home, with the eyes that sparkled in the sky oblivious to his every move.

Jerusalem was not like any other city, but I didn't believe it had been intended for god or man; it was just there because men believed in God, it just so happened to be there. Its presence filled civilization and nature. I was inhabited by the God I didn't believe in, the people I didn't fully belong to, the nation of which I was not a citizen, the parade and celebration tomorrow in which I would be merely a tourist. The sounds of dancing and singing from the shuttered houses

could have been Bastille Day in Paris or Carnival in Port-au-
Prince. But the music was of my tribe, singing and dancing
in Jerusalem at last.

The ancient stone city was now filled with youth, not only
with the inherited rituals. The victory it had inspired to replace the menace of extermination was a triumph over history; the victory belonged to these young people and not to
their ancestors. They wanted to be done with ancestral
purifications through suffering. The monument to the veterans of the Civil War in the Public Square of Cleveland may
once have seemed alive to those who remembered their war.
As a boy I stared at it, finding life only in the pigeons which
covered it. Now I was among those who remembered in their
own bodies; and in the dark city all around me, with its spicy
smells of wine and lamb, its dusty smells of sunbaked stone,
the beautiful Yemenite silversmith was remembering the
war in which she drove a truck, Chaim Hefer was remembering it, Dahn Ben Amotz and Velikansky the actor and Shimon Tal and the men and women of my generation were
remembering. Walking in Jerusalem at four in the morning,
I knew for sure that a metabolic miracle had occurred and
I would never again need rest or sleep.

The surrounding hills turned pale in the filmy increasing
light. The hunched rocks always surprised me by moving.
There were white outcroppings of rock as the dawning began to fill the shadows. And just as I couldn't tell the difference between the sheep and the rocks in the dark of that
night in Jerusalem, though the stars and moon gleamed and
the dry desert air was bright, so often in my own life, I had
made murk of the living and the dead, rage and love, and
confused them in my heart: seeing the dead move as menace,
ignoring the living whom I might have loved.

I walked down the road toward where I didn't live but was

welcome. Because I was still a young man, I defined all my confused feeling as happiness, an uncontainable expulsive energy; it was not quite that; it was a fulfillment and rest expressed as ecstasy; it was just a moment breathing alone under the Judean hills. I had no visions, I saw no fiery god, I heard no voices but the modern ones of city, baby, radio, sink; a shutter shivered shut, dry wood in dry air; I was there and only there, I was I and only I, and this was where I was meant to be. I possessed my soul in a silence which I break with this noise.

I still didn't believe. I remained an American from Lakewood, Ohio. But the tourist had made touch with something in the past which changed him, and more important, changed how he saw everyone else. Just as the slowly moving rocks on the hills in the dawn were not rocks, they were sheep, much that was familiar and ordinary would not be seen as it had been seen before. At that moment some rage in my nature disappeared, and although I do not have secure possession of this reconciliation to fate, I can sometimes call up in time of trouble the sense that it is a fulfillment to live and equally to die. In time of joy I can call on memories that say this too is natural and proper. I did not suddenly learn the faith of my fathers, but I learned the lesson of this faith. It wouldn't shut up my complaining, either, no more than it shut up the complaining of my fathers. But now I also had the reassurance of history which they had given me through their sons and daughters.

"I'll never let you go. I'll never leave you. I'll follow you everywhere," Nachamah had said to me.

"That sounds like a punishment."

"It is. How I'll do it, it is."

But we both were laughing.

Our laughter was like the epileptic's aura before his vision.

I still heard it when I walked the streets of Jerusalem at dawn, in the aura of discovery of history within myself. In the peculiar way to which I had accustomed myself, it remained linked, that faith of my fathers, with my ambiguous faith in girls. There was a steady alive din of morning birds in the air, like the sparrows and robins of the wakeful dawns of my childhood in Lakewood, Ohio. The hunched white outcroppings of rock became whole herds of sheep as the light filled the shadows in the Judean hills. And some of the sheep didn't move, and so these were transformed back into the white rocks which had been turned over by Christian and Saracen, Jew and Roman, by earthquake and the glacial slide of the ages. Jerusalem was golden, just as it had been told! The sun began to rise, a sudden flood of summer sun, and in crazy joy I remembered my own miracle: *I'll never sleep again, I'll never need to sleep again.*

Then I was home and I slept almost immediately. But I was right in one way. There is a kind of sleep, dreams of horror and anxious voyaging, nightmares from sweet Lakewood, Paris, New York, and Port-au-Prince, Army and civilian dreams, with which I was finished. Something for which I had been searching without knowledge had discovered itself to me.

The day was fiery hot, dry, a military day. The city was filled with celebrants for the march-past, fly-by parading and strutting. It seemed years had passed since the night of rock and sheep on chill Judean hills. I had felt triumphantly united with them in predawn loneliness; now, a few hours later, I was isolated from them in the holiday crowd. Waiting in the mob, amid the grandstands, the visitors, the diplomats, the military attachés, I managed a space of calm. Did I like this military May Day? Was this my ideal for humanity, for a people to which I gave my allegiance?

The airplanes roared low.

The tanks stooped and crawled past.

Men waved from turrets; dusty soldiers marched, eyes straight.

Women stood soberly watching, some with tears in their eyes. Another formation of French Mystères flashed overhead. Metal caught the sun; the roar shook the wooden stands. I could have been anyplace just after a war, just before a war.

Was this nation's fate to be no better than any other fate? It had preserved its life through a history of dying. Must it now preserve its life, in a way history has discredited so many times, through the instruments of death? History has discredited that way, but not yet replaced it with another.

Suddenly there was a knot of cheering and applause, and then the knot flowered outward, and the crowd was on its feet, cheering a solemn little man in formal dress, wearing a red sash around his ample middle. "The ambassador of France," Shimon Tal told me. "You see how weak Israel is? Her best friend is France."

And his jolly head creased with laughter, all our friends were laughing, I was laughing. Doubt had moved beyond despair to defiance and this laughter; nothing could bring defeat now, not even degradation and massacre—that too had been tried—nothing but total extermination. And with or without good friends, the people in Jerusalem that day would not go patiently into death.

How I had loved Paris. And when I think of hopeless insecurity, of the best joke about faithlessness, I think of the one whose best friend is France.

In the crowd of diplomats near the French ambassador, a little contrary knot was pushing outward, and I saw a couple trying to make their way through. They were coming toward me. The street reverberated with applause; the French ambassador was bowing and looking about, accepting his due. The couple was still trying to part the crowd, which suddenly gave way. A lady was waving violently at me, her face streaked with tears or sweat, and she was pulling a large, fair, fattish man. The crowd was cheering for France. The lady was waving and shouting my name. It was Hannah Freiberg. Gravely she said, "I want you to meet my husband."

"Shalom," he said. "We have met, Anna. But I wanted to wish you well on this season of celebration."

"Thank you very much."

"I want to say goodbye if I never see you again," Anna Freiberg said to me. She shrugged prettily. "So goodbye."

I think she was determined to embarrass neither me nor her husband. She was proud of him. She had become a woman despite her injuries, as Velikansky became a foolishly ardent young man despite his age, as I became, despite all my history, a Jew returned to Jerusalem. The crowd was singing. There was a buzz of machinery passing, the heavy rumble of warfare in the air. But the mass of people from all over the world, swaying against each other, was singing a chant of deliverance.

Hannah Freiberg had become a woman because of her injuries, as Velikansky was able to become a comic and tragic young man because of his age, as I became a Jew because of my history of withdrawal and evasion of my fate. I too might dedicate a book to the memory of the gypsies, but I was not a gypsy.

Even tonight I would grow drowsy and sleep again. I still resembled my familiar self, though I was dreaming myself into a new life. My fate, which was to become what I was born to be, had provided me with the peculiar necessary choice.

I didn't have to destroy the Unitarian Jewish Temple with its Unitarian rabbi on Euclid Avenue in Cleveland. I simply left it and went off to find perfect freedom through love, literature, and the life of a gypsy free. But now all at once, after several careers, eleven books, a few desperate loves and many which passed the time and a single happy one, some travels and illnesses, some habits which are no longer to be changed, more children than perfect freedom usually intends to sire, I notice that I am a middle-aged American Jewish writer. How can this be? I, who was destined forever to be seventeen, self-created, with a world only to be conquered and all of history waiting ahead of me, find that, while I've slept, much of the future has mysteriously been moved to the past.

In order to understand what remains of the future, I must try to name my ancestors and understand how my separate history came into the language I share with other Americans. The eccentric elements were the inventive half-precisions of immigrant speech: my parents' glancing off English; my father's stubborn use of it as a tool, careless of exactness; my mother's finicky malapropism, picking on words and twisting them to her own purpose. Well, Bergson did that, too. He redefined French to mean what he wanted it to mean; Whitehead also invented words, such as "prehension" and "concretion," meaning only what he meant to mean by them, and generations of students assimilated images of the prehensile monkey's tail catching on to the branch of an idea while the head looked elsewhere. I exchanged letters, and eventually became close friends, with an old newspaperman in Detroit, W.K. Kelsey, who liked my novel *The Man Who Was Not With It* but couldn't understand why I sometimes made up words. I gave him every justification, including Shakespeare, except what I now believe to be the correct one: My parents spoke Yiddish; I invented English freely, as an explorer from Spain invents the Indies in the Caribbean.

But I didn't write dialect, either. I heard my parents and my ear said: Who are these strangers? I heard Cleveland and knew it was supposed to be the correct way. This midwestern flatness made hyperbole shameless and hilarious. I talked like everyone else in suburban playground and tree-shaded street; I also heard the generations of wanderers behind me, whispering in a language which was familiar from the nursery although I never learned to speak it. There must be some funny flashings in the brain as all these signals and expectations are sorted out.

Then, maybe because of this multiple echo, I looked for standards in The Book, every book in sight, all the Scarlet Pimpernels and Three Musketeers, joining the distant company of heroes, until the dream of evasion from my fate turned abstract and philosophic in adolescence. Instead of running away to his cell with the Count of Monte Cristo, I stood in Plato's cave behind the symbolic flames and watched the shadows of reality through language. The romance of instructional nouns. And then, still hoping to conquer the world with my body and pure heart (James Branch Cabell, Thomas Wolfe), I took to logic, aesthetics, ethics, metaphysics. I got from Aristotle, Plato, Bergson, Whitehead, Freud, and their teachers, students, disciples, and enemies, phrases and glints which were tucked away in my head mostly because I thought they were already there, like Shelley's ideas. "Vexed by a dream . . ."—Shakespeare. "Like pearls that through some doge's hands . . ."—Hart Crane. "The secret of unendurable pleasure indefinitely prolonged . . ."—George Sylvester Viereck.

Whatever was on the fly stuck to the flypaper.

But there must be a reason in chemistry, rhythm, meaning, or hope of meaning.

Yiddish and Plato: Well, I wasn't the only one. Delmore Schwartz and Saul Bellow were my elders. I wandered by thumb, then into the Army with tough guys, finding Hemingway and Homer to people my dreams, and Pushkin and Lermontov in a daily routine because the Army needed men to be friendly with the Russians. Then Morningside Heights. Then a new language in France and Haiti, and the playful opening up of Paris student jargon and the Creole of Port-au-Prince. I read Raymond Queneau's *Loin de Reuil*, along with Balzac and Gide. I read the literary essays of Stephane Alexis in a smudged morning daily in Haiti, printed with ancient hand-set type, and voodoo translations from the Greek by my friend Felix Morisseau-Leroy, who was busy destroying his French ancestors with lessons learned from his African ancestors. How complicated it was for Haitians. Haiti was filled with poets who all seemed to be black Jews. Their terrified dream life—conquered by the white man, conquered by their own gods—invaded my own. When I lay abed with malarial hepatitis, I clung to the sound of drums from the hills and the kitchen babble in a pidgin of tongues as if it were a life raft. Amid my desolation of illness, people were still communicating some way. Also, they didn't necessarily need me.

I read French poetry, American novels, a mass of magazines, and the Russian books in which I sought precedents for my own story. I worked at magazine journalism—I liked to travel, I needed the money—and found a rapid notational style to replace the drip-drip-drip of my first novels, stories, and poems. I was less shy than I used to be. I became acquainted with women. I was not afraid to let my hands and feet go where they willed.

The one consistent principle of my time as a writer has been: make mistakes. Others have made mistakes before me, but I claim an original stubbornness in error. The idea is continually to loosen and jiggle thought and intention, and out of the jiggle may appear the free and deep part of a nature. My career has been a series of comebacks after defeats. I wasn't as loose-tongued as Kerouac, nor as tight-fisted as Capote; I was moderately garrulous, keeping my own counsel in public. The mystery of personality is private, and yet that's the writer's public power—he is in touch with mystery. If not in touch, his soul is empty, he is a mere pen-wiggler. If maudlin and self-indulgent, he's a mere celebrity performer, like Judy Garland advertising how hard it is over the rainbow. Many writers in these times have found that the wailing of Judy Garland did not fully satisfy a public avid for confession. They could tell their own sad stories and be petted for it.

In some moods I resolved: words are too precious to waste on anything but the meaning of life, and I wrote nothing, narrow-eyed and parsimonious; my only right was to say what no one else could even imagine. I was alone in the world. I couldn't sleep. I walked alien streets, looking for distraction. I was proud. I was miserable.

Next month I was happier. The parsimonious philosopher was merely selfish, greedily silent, pompous in his isolation. Instead, I was chosen by my sovereign self to pour forth the common hopes and indulge the general dreams—to give pleasure, make funny, pass the time, tell the truth sideways through lies. And out of this nonchalance came words I wanted to bite and sniff, happy improvisations which some-times, alas, made others bite and sniff at the manic impro-viser.

The movements of blood and glands explain much, but they don't explain why some words are magical and others not. Even the vainest writer eventually lies victim of the fact that his heart, lungs, and circulation of blood are very like the pumps and pipes of others. I have found it difficult to write about my books and the portion of my life which has been spent in solitary spaces writing them. I suppose this is be-cause they are still tender, personal, and secret to me, and I mustn't lay retrospective hands on them in composing this narrative. They are encapsulated formulations of my own history, the completed stage on a way, and therefore, even in their imperfections, circled in upon themselves, with their own integrity. I am thinking here about my history as a man and a member of the community of men, not about these secretions from my life which I have called novels and sto-ries. They are the work I do and the dreams I have. My life moves among them and away from them, as the spider moves among and finally away from the web it has spun.

Along with girls, writing, adventure, and distractions, I have sought the answer to a question which is only dimly expressed in the acts of my life. *What is a Jew?* I hardly earned the right to ask it, so much absent as I was from the history of Jews. But it is a specific form of the general question which haunts all of us: Who am I? where are we headed? why have we come from we-know-not-what to die we-know-not-how? Within the silence which surrounds us at both ends of life, what is the significance of our brief and noisy sojourn on earth? I accept the peculiarity of the question. I am left with tribal connections, loyalty to family and perished kin, and must try to begin with these simple matters.

Another question seems paired with my mysterious accident in being born a Jew. What does it mean to be a writer? The writer fits into the Jew who fits into the writer, who fits into the Jew. The interpenetration is continuous. Words, hope of meaning, quest for community, essential choices still to be made; incomplete as a Jew, I am incomplete as a man, and out of this incompleteness, which is also that of a child or a poet, comes the art which demands unity, a continuous labor toward making sense and magic of life. The childish writer begins his career free as a cat, he believes, but in fact governed like the cat by slavery to nature; and if he survives his ignorance, he slyly accommodates to the world, like an old Jew, freed in another way by careless detachment, patient hope, and knowledge that in any case the end of his own time is soon to come. What he keeps is the element of defiance which prevents his being a wise old man like other men. Fact and ideal, history and dream, disappointment and hope, there are no ways to reconcile them but through belief and craft. Mystery overwhelms him. He believes. He does not quite believe. He labors at craft.

Golems, magic rabbis, and furious Hasidic dancing turn me into Instant Anthropologist. I am too empirically American for the mark of lamb fat on the door, although I often have highly satisfactory daymares of my enemies being visited by snail diseases and tropical plagues. "Never again!" applies to ghetto Judaism and bland Jewish Unitarianism, as well as to the fatal periodicity of pogroms. I wish the road were clear. When I was growing up, I felt nothing about the past except an uneasy abstention from history.

Now Jewish history seems fully alive once more. Jewish Unitarianism has been replaced by Jewish rebirth for many who once fled. I've gone away and returned. How to define this road except in negatives? Chicken-soup Judaism, B'nai B'rith and Israel Bond Judaism, country-club Judaism seem mere variations of an American effort to keep busy. The quick element is a responsibility to history, ancestors alive in oneself, a tribal identity with hope, joy, and suffering. That piety is surely not enough. It is only the beginning of a return, a mere recognition, but recognition of possibility is the beginning of possibility. Our isolation of soul is inhabited by a conviction that there must be some community among men with the powers of nature.

To be a Jew leads not to a final definition, but to further questions. No rest in convulsion and conversion. Much of the anxiety, outrageousness, despairing humor, careless burlesque, longing, and nostalgia of American Jewish novelists depends on the puzzle of identity and allegiance in these times. Of course, the class "American Jewish Novelists" is as loose and ambiguous a category as "Southern," "Catholic," or "Black," and the variations of talent and depth make more important classes of their own. But to the extent that we recognize an energy of origin, the class can be named as a factor in the American imagination. There is no excellent beauty which hath not some strangeness in the proportion, Francis Bacon said, and he was no Jewish writer. The persistent search for language and new proportions expresses a search for the fitting identity. *Who am I?* is a question which also asks, From what did I come? To what do I belong?

The tribal answer is only partial: to be at one with a history which continues. Despite what I was told, and especially by the Unitarian rabbi of Cleveland, Judaism is not doctrine, a credo, doing good, marrying a nice girl. It shifts with the times to mean what people make it mean. In this it is like other Eastern religions, which to the European mind are not religions at all. There is a book—but the commentaries are legion. There is only one God, but His name is mystery. Hamlet's question has a simple answer: To be *and* not to be. The peculiar Jewish inheritance, an otherworldly worldliness, offers a vision of the eternal in the here-and-now. The bewildered Mallorcan architect and bullfight judge was also trying as best he could.

"Things standing thus alone shall live behind me," but they also live ahead of me as I let the peculiar Jew within instruct the middle-aged American novelist. Why I am a Jew, why I am a writer, why I am a defrocked adolescent, why I am the father of five, why I am sometimes up and sometimes low, what it bodes to be these things, why so much fun and so much else, how can I nourish myself and the world from these questions in my history—where is the value in the astonishments of life? The puzzles and pleasures which all together make me a writer also make me a Jew. And in moments of faith that there is a possible community out there, they also give the writer moments at one with other strangers on American streets.

14

The Intourist guide who was assigned to me insisted there was no synagogue in Moscow "at this time." Instead, she offered to show me the largest indoor-outdoor swimming pool in the world. Since I had seen the largest indoor-outdoor swimming pool several times, I asked to see a synagogue. Impossible, she said.

I believed it was possible. I dismissed the automobile put at my disposal and asked a cabdriver, in my limping Russian, to take me to the synagogue. No synagogue, he said. Indoor-outdoor swimming pool.

I found an address for the synagogue, picked a place a block away, took a cab to that spot, and then walked to the synagogue. Old men clustered about me and asked questions in Yiddish and Hebrew. I spoke neither language, but had studied Russian. That amazed them. They wondered if I was really a Jew. Could I prove to them, please, that I was really a Jew? They asked if I knew, in Chicago . . . in Los Angeles . . . a cousin in Brooklyn . . . A mob of beards and skullcaps, shrunken bodies, frantic. My school Russian was very halting.

One old man clutched my sleeve, let go, grabbed it again. He had something to say, something he had learned in English, and he wanted to be sure I heard him. He took my sleeve, stubs of fingers were pinching my arm, he made me pay attention in that crowd. He had a marvelous grin, teeth as black and stubby as his fingers amid the tangle of beard, and he got his entire English sentence out in a rush:

"Come out fightin'!"

A few weeks later I was trying to persuade a cabdriver to take me from the internal airport to the international Sheremetevo airport outside Moscow. Only a short time before my flight to Paris. The driver pretended he didn't understand. I groped for the Russian words, but losing patience with his sullen shrugging, said in English, "Hurry up, I'll miss my plane, quickly!"

He put both arms on the wheel, lay his head atilt, and grinned under his peaked cap.

At last, when I suggested going to an official for help if he wouldn't take me, he said with rage, "You spoke Russian well enough, Jew, when you were looking for the synagogue."

Israel again. I returned a few days after the Six-Day War, joined by the person who wanted to meet my friend Shimon Tal and see for herself what Israel meant to her Jewish man from Lakewood, Ohio. An Arab woman looked at my wife, thought she recognized an English lady, and said, "Psst! The Jews did that!"

She was pointing to a crumbled building. She was pointing to a crumbled building which had been constructed with stones from a Jewish cemetery, upon an ancient Jewish cemetery.

We drove past miles and miles of Soviet tanks and trucks, captured intact and waiting to be scrapped or used for training; guns, cannons, ammunition, steel. "Psst! Eenglish!" I said to the lady. "The Jews did that!"

We visited an Egyptian officer's tank. It was luxuriously furnished with rugs, sofa, and teamaker, but no guns. The Israeli captain, shaking his head, said, "We feared it was a secret weapon. Those poor officers. Those poor soldiers led by such officers."

At dawn in Jerusalem, we heard the rhythmic flop of tennis balls. Insomniac Israelis, up at dawn less than a week after the war, were playing tennis, trying to bring their bodies back down to peace. Later in the morning, the bulldozers were at work clearing around the Wailing Wall, the screech of earth-moving equipment much louder than the ritual tears of those come to the beloved city. Arabs watched. Their look was of hatred and fury, and beneath it, pain; and of course the Jewish monuments, cemeteries, and synagogues had been desecrated in East Jerusalem, and now no more of that, but for those dusty men in the street the noise was still a defeat and violation. Victorious Jews were moving in. I was among their company, and remembered what it is to be among the company of losers.

I looked for the circus I had found in 1958—acrobats, animal tamers, sawdust, cotton candy—but of course it was elsewhere now.

My non-Jewish wife studied Hebrew at the Berlitz school in San Francisco after we returned from Israel. I don't speak Hebrew. I can remember certain prayers learned by rote at the Euclid Avenue Temple, but they are not the ones I need. I'll find them.

I thought to be a Jew because I was named so by others. I learned by being one that Jew is more than epithet. The content of tenuous community, risk, and history makes me feel immortal though I'm not. No matter what happens to me, I am continuous with a past which was worthy of better than me; a present when others died to be Jews; a future constructed equally of fate and intention.

— 2 —

On the grounds of a hospital in Biafra, after an air raid by Soviet Migs piloted by East Germans, a little crowd gathered near a rocket still smoking in the turf. The doctors were giving morphine to the hurt and dying spread out on burlap bags. An old man, pushing a bicycle, joined me. "You are from Berkeley?" he asked me.

"San Francisco."

"You think my son is safe in Berkeley? There is trouble there? Rioting?"

"Yes, but I think he's safe."

"You will take him a letter?"

"Yes."

Later, when he brought me the letter, he wanted to talk awhile. He was the sexton in the church of the Fathers of the Holy Ghost at Ihiala, an emaciated old man with a bicycle and a son getting a Ph.D. in biology at the University of California at Berkeley. "We Ibos," he said, "we are known as the Jews of Africa."

"I've heard that."

"Does that mean," he asked, "Biafra will survive?"

— 3 —

Being reduced, as I was, to my name alone still left me with enough. I am. I am Herbert Gold. I am the American Herbert Gold. I am the American Jew Herbert Gold, a writer. I am the Jew who is also an American who remembers he was a Jew raised among people who knew little of what a Jew is. Nor did he know anything.

And I want my children to learn what I finally learned.

As a writer and a man I have sought an impossible consolation in the words *Now I see the truth! Now I embrace it!* In this rush to resolution, the enduring griefs, my own and others, were not always real to me. When I felt sorrow, I felt it at night and waited for the good light of day to drive it off. I worked, I took pleasure, I played against others and against myself. The deepest regrets and pains refuse consolation by truth and embrace. They refuse consolation by any means at all.

I found a peculiar joy in my peculiar allegiance because I needed to join all the lost tribes. Writing and the life of a soldier, student, husband, teacher, father, restless Bohemian, clever organizer in disordered times, all these distractions were not enough. Even the lonely devotion of storytelling becomes part smuggery in isolation. The sorrow written about moves into another world from the sorrow purely suffered. *Now I see the truth!* is a boast. *Now I write the perfect story, meet the perfect girl!* is a blind.

Therefore I have been nervous, erratic, fanciful; I inherit my parents' uninhibited employment of the blundering English language as a tool, a practical device to be explored in mistakes, in the use. Every writer remembers lonely daydreaming from his childhood, and thinks himself shy and withdrawn, both self-created and victimized by family, no matter how public and insistent he becomes in this time of aggressive celebrity. Awareness of Difference and puzzlement about what differences mean compelled my exploration of fantasy, melodrama, play, and manners. Fairly wasteful at times. Detached by fate, I sought to join every flow of feeling with ideas. Not so detached as self-pity might have it, I found myself bound to both Cleveland and Jerusalem, the American idea and the history of Israel, each of them seeking through intention and divine favor a salvation on earth, right now; not in heaven, but today. Or at least tomorrow. Or, please God, next year in Lakewood, Ohio.

The disappointments of history govern a Jewish reluctance to rest in solutions. Neither a responsible style nor a convenient success gives any promise of grasping the meaning of life which writers seek outside of institutional sanction. To be an American writer provides an ambiguous set of pleasures and chagrins. The decisions about life which I have come to might also come to another American writer. But being a Jew gives both ambiguity and secure reference to a passion to put words in order and in disorder, to make clear and unclear, real and magical, practical and pious, in ways not yet known. To clarify the incomprehensible is the deep dream of the novelist. Horror and possibility make him suffer and invigorate him. He reconciles briefly with the unforgivable, and then fills once more with rage and desire. And to the very end of his life, the novelist or the Jew must also leave the mystery intact.

Anxiety and hope are close cousins, related through their common expectation that the future exists. There is no resignation in Judaism. Heaven above is the roof of the house; plenty going on here below, past and future, to keep the mysteries local and at home. That makes it our own business, not God's. No wonder Jews are so nosy and persistent, since there is no pantheon of saints and angels, no tender, ascending Savior. Resignation gets a Jewish fellow noplace. The only truly resigned Jews have been those in such despair that they could only wish for death. That's not resignation. The stony wait for oblivion has no quality of grateful piety in it. But Jews have often found themselves waiting.

And so the survivors are often anxious and hopeful, optimistic and disabused. Clever as Jews are thought to be, they have never succeeded in outsmarting time and place, history and event, the cares of daily life; and in fact, they haven't wanted to. They have suffered without the promise of sweet heaven. They have clung to the notion that human life itself is the great good, provided it can be made better. They are perpetually fretting and trying to show the way. Pious Christians believe that death comes just before dawn, and then they go to heaven. Jews know that death comes at any hour, and then they go noplace. So better do your business today, make plans for tomorrow today, and when tomorrow comes, *if* tomorrow comes, thank God and see if there is still another day likely to follow.

To add to the burden of this total, irreducible value of the individual human life, property is under no circumstance an equivalent to spirit. Historically, what the talion principle meant, eye for eye and tooth for tooth, was that a transgressor could not compensate his victim's heirs by sheep or land, honey or grain. A man's life could not be redeemed by purchase. There is no buying of forgiveness. One thing only was equivalent in value to a man: another man. This is the essential difference between the law of Moses and the code of Hammurabi. It's very severe, too severe for the modern nostalgia for sweet forgiveness, and it, too, cannot face the essential fact of loss: *Nothing* is the equivalent of a man; no grief redeems another grief. But at least it avoids easy redemption. It comes as close as possible to what matters, and it makes that modern nostalgia for sweetness most touching in its effort to find divine mercy. And, too, it helps to explain the ironic Jewish interest in wealth and power for what they are: games, a way of passing the time, a fleeting pleasure, sometimes useful, maybe useful, useful *in case,* second-best and ancillary to a manly life on earth.

When a boy in Lakewood, I turned from the allegiances of unreal history toward a fantastic community in the life of art. When I discovered what that community really was, a community of Manhattan, of property and power, and how it narrows souls, I was blessed to remember that I could still discover the community given me by birthright, a connection someplace. All of us preserve alternatives, no matter how many turnings our roads take. In the light of what the world is, the life of art narrowed toward triviality, while a life joined with the history of my tribe came to parallel my own strivings to write. Much is already printed on the body before we understand anything about ourselves. I must tell what I know and what I don't know, and come to learn more than I have thus far told. And so, partway by this atavism of the Word, I discovered a new way back to the community of writers.

Within my tribal allegiance, the magic and strangeness of its history embracing me, I peer out with longing and wonder at the strangeness and diversity of other stories. Like Jonah speaking from the whale, I speak out of a belly and expect an echo of results. I'm not sure finally if the whale out of which I speak is a Jewish fish or a writer fish; it's both, of course; and the ocean in which it swims includes everyone else, plus everyone's whales.

Being a Jew in the twentieth century is a rigorous infliction and reward. I didn't realize it was also a course of training. History doesn't plan such matters, nor is history to be praised for letting it happen, but gradually a man finds how he has come to be what he is. I set out in middle age with bonds I have discovered, not chosen. My line to the past and future is opened in a way I suspected only lately. There are prayers still to be written for the traditional ceremonies of mourning and celebration. Still Alive—the repeated notation, day after day, in Tolstoy's last journal—is one of the most astonishing claims a man can make. Clear and defiant it is, an essential truth seen to be merely temporary, and heedless, fearful, and accepting, all at once—a complex negotiation with the un-named Judge.

How fine it would be to write my life as if blind and dying, yet in full possession of my soul, in very simple sentences, with no possibility of revisiting the text; to be truthful, and to make the first account of each event sum up the meaning of it, no elaboration necessary, no drama required. Then there would be a pure line leading only to the truth.

Impossible. I can't do that.

And so, to find my truth, what part of it I have been given to find, I have had to think again and elaborate.

And yet it is not very complicated. I now have five chil-dren. I was distressed, not knowing why, by being born a Jew. My life has been fortunate. All it takes to die is to be alive, and all it takes not to die is to remember to live. The first is a permanent truth and the second a temporary one. Absurd-ity and laughter have protected me from clinging to chagrins which were merely mine. Good luck and health have been unmerited gifts from the God in whom I do not believe but who remains a puzzle to me.

My second wife, in whom I believe, is very dear to me. Writing is my other bride. In middle life I have become what I was born, a Jew, and hope my new children, the grand-children of English and Scottish soldiers and merchants, Rus-sian-Jewish merchants and soldiers, Americans, will under-stand how this came to be, since it is also a part of how they came to be, in their turn living and then dying.

— 4 —

If the Jews are the chosen of God to bring the truth of His word onto earth, then how can I be a Jew? I am willing to let

God dictate to me, but He does not speak. Perhaps I am deaf. He is silent.

But if the Jews are a people with continuous pride in their continuous history, then of course I am a Jew. My life has been lived as a function of the holiness of words I cannot pronounce, of wisdom I do not understand, and of the stern morality of a law which I have not followed.

So my being and becoming a Jew are both paradoxes. And yet paradoxes more precious to me than any good and useful idea. Even if we and the world suffer the fate of Biafra, there has been a community in history and some mark of it in seamless time.

I was present at the last birth. My wife and I had done the natural childbirth exercises. We were ready. The doctor was kind and easy.

The child was born, my fourth child, a boy. After three girls, Ann, Judy, and Nina, a boy. We would name him Ari, a Hebrew name meaning the Holy Lion.

"Okay, one more push, Mrs. Gold, Melissa, and it'll be all over. Now push."

She did what she was told. We knew the routine. It was planned and prepared and we understood everything. She pushed and it was not all over.

The doctor's face turned gray.

A baby slipped out into his hands, a tiny, perfectly healthy little boy who had been crouching unnoticed behind his brother Ari all this time, unsuspected by anyone. His cries were piping and powerful. I was crashing about the room, laughing; and also trying to console my wife for this surprise. The doctor was explaining how it could happen, it was logical, it was a surprise, it could easily happen, it happened all the time, this was the first time in all his experience; and I in my sterile white gown was consoling him, too, telling him we didn't mind at all; and my wife and I were consoling the nurses and doctors, telling them not to be upset, they didn't have to predict everything, no one needed to predict and control everything, we were surprised but pleased.

We named him Ethan, because it is an old American name and my wife is descended from Ethan Allen, leader of the Green Mountain boys, and that way we could have one Jewish and one New England Protestant twin. But it turns out that Ethan is also an ancient Hebrew name, spelled Aleph Yod Tav Nun and meaning Firmness, Perpetuity, and Strength.

Having a child, now that I have had five, does not seem to be a creative act. It's an act in which I assist nature to be creative. I enjoy a power which is not mine but in which I share.

Being a Jew has come to seem like having a child: I have given birth to the Jewishness within myself. I did not choose it; it has been given me; but I share in the power and pain which it has offered. I am a part of history, not merely a kid on a street corner or a man making out okay. The suffering of others is mine, too.

During much of my earlier smiling life, I thought I might go smiling out of my mind, and despite the modern fad for madness, it did not delight me. I covered my fears with smiles. I smiled to tell the world how sweet I would be. I made jokes to tell the world I was agreeable about things; it could trust me; I didn't care; I might be rash, but no trouble at all, sir.

Later in life, most men learn to limit their desires and dreads, and this we take for wisdom. What begins as wisdom ends, I see from other aging men, in melancholia and worse. But I am not sorry to lose the fear of madness, and as I connect myself with the history of my tribe, I know that I cannot merely die; I belong with my father, with the man with acromegaly, with Schneider and Tal, and perhaps if I'm lucky, also with the gypsies. Just as I'm not entirely sure of what it means to be a father, except that it means some joys and some responsibilities, some risks, terrors, and exaltations, so I'm not sure what my destiny as a Jew means—or what the destiny of the Jews means—except that it is a unique fate, a peculiar devotion to world and spirit wrapped together. And that I have at last become what I was when my Old Country father and mother in Cleveland submitted to nature and conceived me.